● 2023年上海师范大学天华学院硕士学位授予单位提早培育计划
（项目编号：Z30006.23.103）

高校英语教学优秀设计案例：
新思路、新启示

● 胡雅楠　胡玥　卜迅　编著

苏州大学出版社
Soochow University Press

图书在版编目(CIP)数据

高校英语教学优秀设计案例：新思路、新启示/胡雅楠，胡玥，卜迅编著. --苏州：苏州大学出版社，2024.7. -- ISBN 978-7-5672-4854-0

Ⅰ．H319.3

中国国家版本馆CIP数据核字第2024C8W427号

| 书　　　名：高校英语教学优秀设计案例：新思路、新启示
| 编 著 者：胡雅楠　胡　玥　卜　迅
| 责任编辑：沈　琴
| 装帧设计：刘　俊
| 出版发行：苏州大学出版社(Soochow University Press)
| 社　　　址：苏州市十梓街1号　邮编：215006
| 印　　装：广东虎彩云印刷有限公司
| 网　　　址：www.sudapress.com
| 邮　　　箱：sdcbs@suda.edu.cn
| 邮购热线：0512-67480030
| 销售热线：0512-67481020
| 开　　　本：787 mm×1 092 mm　1/16　印张：8.5　字数：218千
| 版　　　次：2024年7月第1版
| 印　　　次：2024年7月第1次印刷
| 书　　　号：ISBN 978-7-5672-4854-0
| 定　　　价：36.00元

凡购本社图书发现印装错误，请与本社联系调换。服务热线：0512-67481020

序言 Preface

  推进"一带一路"建设、推动中华文化走出去等国家决策部署,凸显了英语专业在日益频繁的国际交流中的重要地位,也为英语专业的发展创造了新的发展机遇。《国家中长期教育改革和发展规划纲要(2010—2020年)》拉开了英语专业新一轮的教学改革帷幕。面对学生思辨缺席、教学质量滑坡等种种问题,上海师范大学天华学院自2016年开始活力课堂教学改革,目前已经进行了七轮,教学模型也已经更新到2.0版。活力课堂包括"课前—课中—课后"完整的教学环节,由传统的以教师为中心转化为以学生为中心,教师精心组织的合作性、探索性学习,通过课堂互动、独立思考、小组讨论、问题辩论等方法,提高学生学习的主动性、积极性,以及思考问题的独立性和批判性,实现高认知度和高参与度的教学。

  在活力课堂的教学改革过程中,教师坚持以赛促教,在参加各种高规格的教学比赛中创新教学设计,打磨教学技能,改进教学方法,并将参赛所学积极应用于教学实践,切实提升教学效果。综合之前关于高校英语专业课程教学设计的文献,多数学者聚焦理论原则的探讨、教学模型的建构以及实证研究的开展,但是基于教师一线教学的真实设计案例的相关研究,则比较少见。基于此,本书以"综合英语""高级英语""口译理论与实践"三门核心课程为例,基于主讲教师一线教学实践,集中展示了生动翔实的教学设计案例。本书选取的三门课程建设历史悠久,基础深厚,主讲教师均有十五年以上的高校教学经验,并多次在高规格教学比赛中斩获佳绩,专家评价好,学生满意度高。

  "综合英语"是英语专业一、二年级的专业基础课,在课程体系中处于核心地位。教学对标《普通高等学校本科外国语言文学类专业教学指南》,融语言、文学、翻译和文化于一体,强调听、说、读、写、译技能的全面发展,用经典题材深挖中西方历史和文化,用当下话题反映社会关切。课程融综合文化素养于语言学习之中,重在提升有效语言输出能力,培养跨文化能力、思辨能力、协作能力和学习能力,注重语言课程的价值养成。作为上海高校市级一流本科课程和上海市课程思政示范课程"综合英语"的负责人,主讲教师胡玥摘得第二届上海高校青年教师教学竞赛二等奖、第三届上海市高校教师教学创新大赛二等奖、第三届"外教社杯"全国高校外语教学大赛上海赛区二等奖、第六届上海市民办高校教师教学技能大赛特等奖、第七届全国高等院校英语教师教学基本功大赛一等奖、外研社"教学之星"大赛全国总决赛二等奖、第二十七届韩素音青年翻译奖竞赛全国一等奖等,并获得上海市巾帼建功标兵、上海市教育系统三八红旗手等荣誉称号。

"高级英语"是英语专业高年级的核心课程,通过细分教学目标、落实思辨设计、有效使用教材、数智赋能教学,致力于促进学生语言知识技能、思辨人文素养和价值品格塑造的协同发展,引导学生将思维培养入脑、价值传递入心、文化传播入手。作为上海市级重点课程和上海市课程思政示范课程"高级英语"的负责人,主讲教师卜迅曾获第三届上海高校青年教师教学竞赛三等奖、外研社"教学之星"大赛全国总决赛二等奖、第七届全国高等院校英语教师教学基本功大赛一等奖、高等学校外语课程思政优秀教学案例征集活动上海市一等奖及全国高校外语微课大赛上海赛区二等奖。

"口译理论与实践"结合了口译行业发展前沿,对课程教学内容进行持续改进,完善了智慧教学模式。通过技术支持,课前能精准记录学生各类学习疑难,课上能及时调整反馈。五大主题篇章和六大口译技巧专题将线上学习的自主性、课堂教学的互动性、实践教学的探索性和课外学习的拓展性有机结合起来,科学提升了学习广度和深度。主讲教师胡雅楠作为2023年上海高校市级一流本科课程"口译理论与实践"的负责人,曾摘得2022年第五届上海高校青年教师教学竞赛一等奖、第七届全国高等院校英语教师教学基本功大赛二等奖、外研社"教学之星"大赛全国总决赛二等奖,并荣获2022年上海市教学能手、上海市教育系统巾帼建功标兵等称号。

希望本书中的教学设计案例能为高校英语专业同类课程的教学设计提供新思路,带来新启示。由于编者水平有限,书中难免会有不足之处,也请各位读者不吝赐教,批评指正。

目录

第一章 教学设计思路点拨

1. Book 1 Unit 4 My Forever Valentine / 003
2. Book 4 Unit 2 Space Invaders / 010
3. Book 6 Unit 11 My Wood / 015
4. Educational Interpreting：Ceremonial Speeches / 021

第二章 "综合英语"教学设计

1. Book 4 Unit 1 Never Give In, Never, Never, Never (1) / 033
2. Book 4 Unit 1 Never Give In, Never, Never, Never (2) / 038
3. Book 2 Unit 7 The Jeaning of America / 043
4. Book 4 Unit 6 The Discus Thrower (1) / 048
5. Book 4 Unit 6 The Discus Thrower (2) / 053

第三章 "高级英语"教学设计

1. Book 6 Unit 1 A Class Act / 059
2. Book 6 Unit 2 Bards of the Internet / 065
3. Book 6 Unit 9 How to Grow Old / 074
4. Book 5 Unit 1 The Fourth of July / 082
5. Book 5 Unit 3 A Hanging / 087
6. Book 5 Unit 5 Superstition / 090

第四章 "口译理论与实践"教学设计

1. Educational Interpreting: Astronomy Photographer of the Year / 095
2. Business Interpreting: Olympic Economy / 099
3. Business Interpreting: E-sports / 104
4. Cultural Interpreting: Du Fu / 109
5. Cultural Interpreting: Father of Hybrid Rice / 116
6. Cultural Interpreting: Buzzwords / 122

第一章

教学设计思路点拨

1. Book 1 Unit 4 My Forever Valentine

课程名称：综合英语	
教学对象：英语专业一年级学生	
学时安排：1 学时	
教学目标： ✓ 知识目标：理解文章的基本脉络和主旨 ✓ 技能目标：掌握记叙文的基本阅读方法，学会概括文章大意 　　　　　　学会对比中西方父母之爱表达方式的异同 ✓ 情感目标：理解爱的不同表达方式	
教学重点： 记叙文的基本要素；作者情感变化背后的隐含意义；课文中的"父亲"形象	
教学难点： 中西方父母之爱表达方式的异同	

教学过程	设计说明
一、课前准备 1. 学习通平台观看视频 *What Asian Parents Don't Say*（时长 3 分钟）。 2. 讨论并回答问题。 Q1：Have your parents said "I love you" to you? Q2：How do they express their love to you? Give one example. 3. 对讨论中的发言进行总结，并准备 1 分钟的课堂汇报。	网上课程视频直观呈现了包括中国父母在内的亚洲父母不善表达的刻板形象，帮助学生熟悉本单元主题。讨论板块的思考题启发学生结合自身经历反思父母表达关爱的方式，学生还需要对讨论板块的发言进行汇总。**这些课前活动为课中教学做好准备。**
二、课中教学（共 45 分钟） （一）导入环节（5 分钟） 1. 由标题引发提问，检查学生课文预习情况。 Q1：Who is the author's valentine? Q2：Why does the author call him her valentine? 2. 回顾课前讨论任务，学生汇报调查结果。	**导入环节**检查预习情况，由此引出父母之爱的话题。学生汇报展示是对网上讨论的回顾，旨在锻炼学生分析数据的

3. 播放 *Asian Parents React to I Love You* 视频片段，以提问启发学生反思自己向父母表达爱意的方式。 Q1：Have you said "I love you" to your parents? Q2：How do you think they would react if you just said it out of the blue?	能力和口头表达能力。在课堂上讨论子女向父母表达爱意的方式是对本单元主题的深化。
（二）课文讲解（35分钟） 1. 体裁+结构分析。（15分钟） Q：How to read a piece of narration? Who was/were involved in the event? [Character(s)] When and where did the event occur? [Setting] ⎫ What happened? (Action) ⎬ main idea How are the events arranged in the story? (Order) ⎭ What's the point of view of the narration? What's the theme of the story? 　　引导学生关注记叙文的基本要素（人物、时间、地点、事件、顺序等），掌握记叙文阅读方法。请同学从课文中找出这些要素，并学会利用基本要素概述大意。 （1）分析人物要素和相关细节。 ➢ **WHO**：my father 　His hobby：<u>watching football games</u> Evidence 1：The traditional holidays in our house when I was a child were spent **timing elaborate** meals around football games. 词汇 elaborate e. g. The _____ cooking methods are _____ in the cookbook. elaborate：*a.* detailed and complicated *v.* to explain in detail Evidence 2：My father **tried to** make pleasant chitchat and eat as much as he could during half time. 　His work：<u>office work</u> 　His favorite holiday：<u>Valentine's Day</u>	由于本节课是本单元的第一次课，学生需要在细读文本前了解文章结构。我们以记叙文体裁为切入点，通过梳理记叙文的基本要素，并在文中找出相应的短语或句子作为依据的方法，帮助学生建立起对文章基本脉络的认识，掌握记叙文的基本阅读方法。

Evidence: But he didn't truly **shine** until Valentine's Day. 提示学生思考 shine 的内涵意义：shine 原指太阳或其他光源发光发亮，在本文中，指父亲过节的热情只有在情人节时才会真正显露出来。既暗示父爱如阳光一般炽热，又让人想象出他由内而外的喜悦之情。 （2）分析场景要素。 ➢ **WHAT**: offering her valentines ➢ **WHEN**: on each Valentine's Day （3）关注时间线索词。 ➢ **ORDER**: chronological order **Time indicators** Para. 3: ... when I was six Para. 5: As I grew older ...　　　　　　chronological Para. 7: ... on the Valentine's Day eight　　　　order years ago **Main idea**(who + what + when + order) Q: What is the story narrated in the text about? A: The text <u>recollects</u> (order) a series of events concerning <u>the narrator's father</u> (who), who <u>showed his love</u> (what) for his daughter by <u>offering her valentines</u> (what) on <u>each Valentine's Day</u> (when). （4）分析叙述视角。 Point of the view: the first-person point of view narration ⇒ the author's feelings 2. 主题分析。（20 分钟） ➢ 学生讨论：将全班同学分为三组，以小组讨论的方式分别思考作者回忆的三个事件中收到的礼物是什么、心情如何以及作者为什么会有这样的心情。提示学生关注作者的心情变化。	在梳理基本要素的基础上，帮助学生概述文章大意。 引导学生关注第一人称叙述视角下叙述者的情感，由此转入主题分析。

Scenario	Valentines	Her feelings	Why
… when I was six	a ring with a piece of red glass; a card signed "Love, Dad"	wearing that ring with a pride that all the cards in the world can't surpass	
As I grew older …	heart-shaped boxes of chocolates; a card signed "Love, Dad"	becoming more of a perfunctory response	
… eight years ago	a card signed "Love, Dad"	putting a lump in my throat	

主题分析以小组讨论的方式进行,学生需要关注三个事件中作者收到的礼物是什么、心情如何,并思考作者为何会有这样的心情,其中为何会有这样的心情是分析的重难点。情感变化主线的分析为揭示本文主题做好铺垫。

Scenario 1

➢ 词汇讲解

surpass: *v.* to be better than

e. g. Her excellent performance surpassed all our expectations.

Scenario 2

➢ 词汇讲解

give way to: to be replaced by

◇ He was not the man to give way to this kind of pressure.
◇ Drivers have to give way to traffic coming from the right.
◇ She gave way to a burst of crying.
◇ As he became ruder and ruder, Bob's discomfort gave way to anger.

- allow oneself to be overcome by an emotion
- yield to
- be replaced by
- allow sb. or sth. to go first

具体到每一场景的分析,由于本节课不属于文本细读,因此教学只涉及理解作者情感脉络必须解决的难句和词汇,目的是教授学生应对词汇的一般方法。

Q: What did the author think of the gifts? The cards seemed less important. I took for granted the valentine that would always be there. "Love, Dad" just didn't seem quite enough. ⎫⎬⎭ perfunctory attitude	这些问题可以引导学生关注作者情感变化背后的根源。学生在回答问题时,一定要从文中找到相应的论据进行论述佐证。

➤ 思考问题

Q1: Why didn't the "Love, Dad" card and gift seem quite enough to the author?

A: As she grew older, the author had placed her hopes and dreams on receiving cards and gifts from other people, who she thought were more important to her than her father was.

Q2: Did the father know he was replaced? Did he feel disappointed? What did he do?

A: He obviously knew he was replaced and very likely he felt disappointed, but he never let it show. What's more, when he found his daughter was disappointed over valentines that didn't arrive for her, he would try much harder to create a positive atmosphere, doing whatever he could to make her day a little brighter.

Scenario 3

➤ 思考问题

Q: Describe the last valentine the author received from her father and figure out its implied meaning.

	The last valentine	Implied meaning
What	a card only	Although he was too sick to go out to buy a real gift, he still tried as much as he could to show his love to his daughter.
Price	inexpensive	
Where he bought it	from door-to-door charity project	
Signature	barely illegible handwriting "Love, Dad"	

通过描述最后一次情人节礼物的特点,分析它与之前礼物的差异和差异背后的隐藏含义,学生可以明白为何一份普通的礼物会让作者哽咽。

分析至此,文章的主题已经不言自明。作者以自己情感的变化为主线印证了父爱的无私与伟大。

Q: Why did the last valentine put a lump in her throat? A: Because this was the last gift she would receive from her father. Although he was seriously ill, he still tried as much as he could to express his love to her. The last gift was a reminder of her father's profound love and it also made her know that she had a father who continued a tradition of love with a generosity of spirit. ▶ 学习通在线讨论 由同学在网上讨论板块输入关键词，并现场简要阐释理由。 What kind of father do you think he is?	该问题是对课文主题分析的总结，有一定难度，但**通过在线互动的方式**，学生可以先找关键词，再找理由丰富论点，**在同学们的通力合作下**，文中父亲的形象慢慢丰满起来。
（三）总结＋作业布置（5分钟） 1. 文化对比：结合导入环节，对比文中的父亲与中国父母在爱意表达方式上的异同。请学生讨论： Do you want to hear those important words from your parents or are you comfortable with receiving their message of love without being said? 2. （课后探索）作业布置：根据中西方父母异同的讨论绘制思维导图。	在总结文中父亲形象的基础上进行**文化对比**，这是**对导入环节的呼应**，由此本节课的教学形成整体性设计。此处设计了追问环节，目的是引导学生**真正认识中国父母之爱，而不是狭隘地认同或反对**。课后学生需要将本节课的讨论内容绘制成思维导图，这有助于他们反思课堂教学，并为完成最后的"大任务"奠定基础。

板书设计

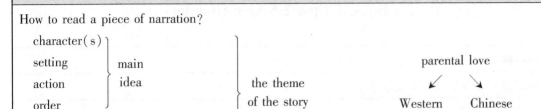

How to read a piece of narration?

教学反思

  本单元设计围绕"爱的表达和理解"的"大观念"(Big Idea)展开教学,通过多模态任务,引导学生比较不同文化背景下父母之爱表达方式的异同,启发学生对父母之爱进行深层次思考,并最终完成"我眼中的中国父母"的"大任务"(Big Project),展现中国父母的真实形象。

  本次教学设计是本单元的第一次课。课程教学从课前准备到课中教学到课后反思都能对"大观念"一以贯之,引导学生在理解课文的基础上结合自身经历进行文化对比分析,形成整体性课程设计。导入从视频着手,结合学生自身体验展开讨论,不仅充分调动了学生的积极性,还使得他们能够利用已有知识框架展开论述。课中的结构和主题分析旨在帮助学生掌握文章基本脉络,建立起对主题的基本认识,在此基础上,总结环节的文化对比和分析也就水到渠成、顺理成章。整体教学设计做到了理论联系实际,也能通过案例教学、课堂讨论、课后拓展等形式多样的活动安排培养学生的自主学习能力、团队合作能力和家国情怀。

2. Book 4 Unit 2 Space Invaders

课程名称：综合英语
教学对象：英语专业二年级学生
学时安排：1学时
教学目标： ✓ 知识目标：掌握与课文相关的语言表达 　　　　　理解文章第一段的主旨大意 ✓ 技能目标：掌握描写片段的写作技巧 ✓ 情感目标：了解有关个人空间的文化差异 　　　　　理解在公共场合尊重个人空间的重要性
教学重点： 词汇的隐含意义；具体词（specific words）和概括词（general words）的区别；利用具体词和修辞手法进行描写（写作技巧）
教学难点： 有关个人空间的文化差异

教学过程	设计说明
一、课前准备 　　学习通布置调查任务：以"How close is too close"为主题调查日常生活中大家对个人空间的感受和反应。	课前准备与课中教学导入部分的讨论一脉相承，课中视频和讨论进一步深化学生对个人空间概念的认识，课后作业引入文化对比，为个人空间的解读增添跨文化视角，从而形成整体性教学设计。
二、课中教学（共45分钟） （一）导入环节（8分钟） 1. 由标题引出个人空间的概念，带领学生集体讨论以下问题。 Q1：What is personal space?	导入环节侧重训练听说能力。首先从标题入手引出个人空间概念，结合学生日常体验组织讨论，提升学生的课堂参与度。

Q2: How would you feel if you're in a crammed situation? Q3: What would you do if someone in the elevator is too close to you? 2. 播放视频 *How Close Is Too Close*，完成填空。 Most simply _____ away. This guy even _____. But several decided to _____ their ground. I went toe-to-toe with this woman, and she wouldn't _____. And this woman who stayed pressed against the back of the elevator may have remained _____, but she felt something very _____. "I had a moment when I was kind of wanting to _____ you, or shove you or punch you or _____ at you." 3. 集体讨论：个人空间的重要性。 （二）课文讲解（30分钟） 1. 播放录音，提出以下问题供学生思考。 Q1: Who were those people in the line? Q2: What was the shape of the original line? Q3: What happened to the line? 2. 利用以上问题引导学生细读第一段，掌握基本脉络。 Q1: Who were those people in the line? A: a man in a sweat-suit → the author → a woman reading *Wall Street Journal* → a man **scribbling** a check → a white-haired lady 词汇 scribble: *v.* to write sth. carelessly or hurriedly Q2: What was the shape of the original line? A: The line was **snaking** around some **tired** velvet ropes. 词汇① snake (*vt. /vi.*): to move in long twisting curves e.g. The road snaked its way up and down the hill. ② tired: *a.* slackened	视频能让学生直观感受个人空间被入侵带来的负面影响，在主题上也能**呼应课前准备布置的任务**，加深了学生对课前任务的认知和理解。 在语言技能层面，所填词汇均为表达动作和心情的具体词（specific words），契合了本节课**运用具体词进行描写**的**教学重点**。 本节课是对课文第一段的分析，强调文本细读，引导学生**从 what 和 how 两大层面理解课文大意**，并能够归纳出重要的写作技巧。 具体来说，一方面通过三个问题帮助学生厘清课文的基本脉络，同时穿插重点词汇的讲解；另一方面以小组合作学习的方式，层层引导，最终让学生明白本段在描写层面的精妙之处。

Q3：What happened to the line? A：We were all **hugger-mugger** against each other. The original lazy line **collapsed** in on itself **like a slinky**. 词汇① hugger-mugger：*a.* disorder ② collapse：*v.* to break apart and fall down suddenly 修辞分析 like a slinky：simile（rhetorical device） e.g. My love is like a red, red rose. e.g. Bolt runs as fast as cheetah. 3. 分组任务：将学生分成六组，找出本段中描写人物动作和心情的单词或短语，思考其隐含意义。 ● Tasks for Groups 1 – 4：Find out and act out what these people did. ● Tasks for Groups 5 & 6：Find out how they felt. 4. 请学生找出本段中描写人物动作的单词或短语并表演，带领学生讨论人物为何会有这些动作。 ● inch toward：to move slowly and carefully ● minutely advance toward：to move forward toward … carefully ● sidle up to：to move close to sb. or sth. slowly and quietly, as if you don't want to be noticed ● shuffle toward：to walk very slowly or noisily, without lifting your feet off the ground 5. 请学生找出本段中描写人物情绪的单词或短语，带领学生讨论为什么人物会有这样的心情。 ● in his eagerness ● embarrassed ● in mild annoyance ● absent-mindedly 6. 思考：What will be lost if all these verbs and verbal phrases are replaced by the general word "walk"? 7. 总结本段的写作技巧。	讨论隐含意义是本节课的教学重点之一，这样才能使学生理解描写文中 specific words 和 general words 的区别所在。 表演能让学生进一步体会具体词的传神之处。 情绪词的讨论揭示了公众场合侵犯个人空间带来的连锁反应，印证了 "Bad manners are infectious"，由此点明在公共场合尊重彼此个人空间的重要意义。

（三）拓展练习（5分钟） 1. 示范本文写作技巧在描写文中的应用。 e. g. people who are trying to get out of the lift <u>revised edition</u>: riders wedging themselves out just before the door closes 2. 请学生根据示例改写下列句子。 e. g. people crossing the street <u>revised edition</u>: pedestrians zigzagging through the traffic e. g. people moving forward <u>revised edition</u>: passengers pressing forward like fidgety taxis at red light	拓展练习侧重于对写作技巧的培养。在归纳写作技巧的基础上，通过实例示范其运用。学生操练所学技巧，达到语言输入服务于语言输出的目的。
（四）布置作业（2分钟） 1. Employ the strategies discussed here to write a short paragraph that describes your experience of personal space invasion.	作业1要求学生模仿作者的写作手法，写一段个人空间遭入侵的体验。该任务可以帮助学生围绕教学重难点进一步反思，内化所学技巧，实现语言输入为语言输出服务的最终目标。
2. （课后探索）学习通布置：Reflect upon the video watched in class and add cultural perspective to your survey results.	作业2是对课前准备阶段布置任务的升华，是在课堂视频讨论的基础上引入的文化视角，丰富了学生对个人空间的认知。

板书设计

1. What is personal space?
2. How would you feel if you're in a crammed situation?
3. What would you do if someone in the elevator is too close to you?

What the text says

1. Who were those people in the line?
2. What was the shape of the original line?
3. What happened to the line?

How the text says

教学反思

本单元设计围绕"文明举止"的"大观念"(Big Idea)展开教学,通过多模态任务引导学生在习得语言的同时从个人空间角度理解公共场合文明举止的重要性,启发学生对个人空间代入文化差异的深层次思考,达到课程思政教育的目的。

本节课教学一共分为三部分。第一部分通过标题引出概念,结合学生日常体验展开讨论,在此基础上完成视频任务,让学生深入了解个人空间的重要意义,这也是对课前布置的调研任务"How close is too close"的呼应。第二部分围绕第一段课文从两方面展开分析:在What层面设计的三大问题循序渐进地串起了第一段的整体分析,帮助学生理解文章脉络和主旨;在How层面的探索主要通过小组协作讨论的方式进行,目的是充分调动学生参与课堂讨论的积极性。任何语言输入,其目的都是语言输出。第三部分重点操练了两大写作技巧,实现了语言输入服务于语言输出的最终目标。作业1是课堂操练的升级版。经过课堂学习,学生对于课前所做的调查有了更多文化上的思考,在此基础上作业2有关文化视角的切入也就水到渠成了。

本课程设计秉承人本主义教学理念,主要强调教学内容上的两大聚焦。

一是聚焦学习者。通过形式多样的教学活动,如视频练习、小组讨论、表演等,关注学习者的人格素质培养和英语听、说、读、写技能的同步提升,培养协作能力和自主学习能力。

二是聚焦文本。引导学生进行细致的文本分析,从重点词汇的讲解过渡到文章脉络的把握,最后上升到写作技巧的归纳,让学生真正做到学有所思、思有所得、得有所用,培养学生的批判性思维能力,并最终由内容上的两大聚焦上升为对东西方文化个人空间概念异同的比较,提高学生的跨文化理解能力。

3. Book 6 Unit 11 My Wood

课程名称：高级英语	
教学对象：英语专业三年级学生	
学时安排：4 学时	
教学目标： ✓ 知识目标：掌握财产占有对人的心理影响的相关表达 　　　　　　识别文中所用的修辞手法——典故 ✓ 技能目标：分析和比较中西方典故中的财产观，进行跨文化阐释 　　　　　　结合社会热点进行案例分析和观点评价 ✓ 情感目标：反思财产占有和幸福感之间的关系 　　　　　　辩证思考消费主义现象，追求积极的生活方式和获得精神上的满足	
教学重点： 财产占有对人的心理影响的相关表达；文中所用的修辞方法及写作策略	
教学难点： 典故的概念、语篇功能及跨文化比较	

教学过程	设计说明
一、课前准备 **上传学习资料和任务单，启动在线讨论。** 1. 教师围绕"财产占有"这一文章主题，将补充资料"Of Avarice, Appetite, a Rich Life with Less Stuff, Danshari"上传至课程章节和资源板块，供学生课前自主阅读。 2. 学生收听访谈音频，观看 TED 讲座，并完成相关的词汇填空练习。 （1）*Phenomenon* —_____ therapy, cure for pressure —_____ consumption *Question* —Feel _____ or ashamed over our shopping? —Is ownership the highest form of self-_____? —To _____ or not to _____?	通过补充与课文主题相关的阅读材料，提供不同的视角，鼓励学生从多个角度对语篇进行解读。 教师选取一段电台访谈节目的音频，让学生带着问题去听，抓住关键信息，加强语言知识的输入和储备，为之后的语言输出练习做准备。

（2）*Surgeon*—*a dilemma* —Keep buying ＿＿＿＿ —Stop buying ＿＿＿＿ —*Schizophrenia*：to save economy or planet? （3）*Psychologist*—*I* ＿＿＿＿ *what I buy.* —I look good in my world —I work hard —I pay my taxes （4）*Religious writer*—＿＿＿＿ *with less possession.* —Less to maintain —Less to dust —More ＿＿＿＿ 3. 教师发布线上问卷，了解学生的财产观。 4. 教师选取一段关于极简主义的 TED 演讲，让学生总结主讲人的观点，并在讨论板块设置思考题：如果是你，拥有百万年薪，是否会放弃眼前的一切，做出同样的选择？ 5. 学生课前观看微课《你所不知道的典故》，完成自主学习表。	三位嘉宾谈及了各自的财产观，使学生听到不同的声音，接受多元的观点，保持开放和包容的文化态度。 将学生置于情境之中，促使其深入思考。 针对课文中的文化难点——典故这种修辞写作手法，教师录制微课视频，供学生课前自主学习，从而使上课更加有的放矢，提高效率。
二、课中教学 1. 导入：头脑风暴 & 苏格拉底式提问。 Q1：What pops up in your mind when it comes to property? Q2：What does property mean to you? Q3：What is the author's property in the text? Q4：How does his answer to the question differ from yours? Q5：Do you agree with the author? Do you have similar worries or concerns as the author?	采用启发式教学法，通过苏格拉底式提问，循序渐进地启发学生对语篇的理解和对主题的思考。 基于学生回答顺势发问，引导学生联系自身经历和实际，展开联想，对作者观点不盲从，从而培养学生的思辨能力。

2. 文本分析：思维导图、小组汇报、工作表。 学生根据自主学习表进行小组讨论，同时就一些困惑的地方提出疑问。比如词汇层面，学生找出了 kingdom of Heaven、robe of God、bath in Jordan、bishop、pulpit、Son of Man、sinister trinity 等具有丰富文化内涵的词语，并结合自己查找的资料进行了解释。	课堂活动任务设计致力于促进学生的认知、情感和行为投入，当学生以良好的状态投入学习时，会积极参与任务，不断思考，并享受学习的过程，从而实现春风化雨的"隐性"思政教育。
学生提出以下问题：为什么作者买了小树林，其他人会"participate in my shame"？教师答疑解惑，并进行追问： ——在中国文化中有与 asceticism 对应的概念吗？ ——作者的人生经历对其观点有何影响？ ——作者的哪句引言呼应了其文本的观点？	采取任务式教学方式，教师根据教学目标及环节设计相应的自主学习表，内容层层递进，有梯度，使学生"忙起来"，有效提高学生的课堂参与度。 针对学生的提问，教师通过启发和引导进行解答，并对一些重要的文化知识点进行补充和追问。
对于作者提出的第二点"endlessly avaricious"，老师进行一连串的发问： —Why does the author mention the furniture? —Do you agree with the author? Why or why not? —Are you satisfied with what you have? —How does your personal experience echo the author's point?	通过启发式提问，教师引发学生联想，鼓励学生结合自身经历，将来自作品的认识和体验与现实世界连接，与作者产生跨越时空的共情。
此话题引起了学生的热烈讨论，他们提出："To conform to the classic style, I also need to buy the fine jewelry and the luxury handbag. And the shabby home is no longer the right place for a lady wearing such a fancy dress."由此得出结论："People will never be satisfied. They always want more."正可谓"欲壑难填"，而这正好呼应了作者的观点："endlessly avaricious"。	小组讨论时鼓励学生提问，挑战权威，追求真理，教师则负责答疑解惑，形成知识共建、合作探究的积极的课堂氛围。

3. 写作策略赏析：看图说话、中国故事、文化对比。 **看图说话**：由一组学生担任文化讲解员，根据教师提供的图片和关键词，向其他同学讲解文中这两个典故的文化内涵，并探讨这些典故是如何服务于作者观点的。	采取交际式教学法，针对文化难点 stout man & slim camel，Ahab & Naboth，教师设置了不同的文化交际任务。通过讲解，学生实现了知识的内化，也更好地了解了作者的观点："Property makes people heavy and greedy."。
用英语讲中国故事：学生需要用英语阐释中国文学典故中所体现的财产观，并和文中的财产观进行跨文化比较。同学们引经据典，有的引用名家名言"不义而富且贵，于我如浮云"，指出中国文人"视金钱如粪土"的价值观；还有学生列举"良田千顷不过一日三餐，广厦万间只睡卧榻三尺""箪食瓢饮，不改其乐""斯是陋室，惟吾德馨"等诸多反映中国古人财产观及生活方式的诗句，与文中作者的观点形成了跨文化呼应。	在将中华文化典故翻译成英文时，学生有意识地将文中所学和财产相关的语言表达及修辞手法运用其中，达成有效输出，成功对接了语言知识目标，同时培养了文化传播意识，实现了语言、技能和价值塑造的协同发展。
还有的同学找到中国神话故事《封神演义》中商纣王象牙筷子的故事。这个中文典故刚好呼应作者第四段中的圣经典故：亚哈王出于贪心想要买下拿伯的葡萄园，最终其皇后将拿伯害死。	鼓励学生从中外比较的视角进行深入阐释，探索各自背后隐藏的文化原因，并进行批判性审视，强调对文化的普遍性概念的深刻理解，提高跨文化思辨素养。
4. 主题探讨：案例分析、课堂展示、同伴互评。 教师以"购物狂欢节""买买买"的现象作为案例，让学生分析消费主义背后的心理成因，并讨论"Do possessions make you happy?"。	采取研究型教学法，要求学生针对当下有争议性的热点话题，使用学过的方法进行案例分析，发掘现象背后的原因，提出可行建议。

有同学结合第六单元文中句子"buy a new life and fill the vacancy"对消费主义进行解读;有同学引用奥斯卡·王尔德(Oscar Wilde)的金句"人生有两大悲哀",指出大量同类物品的堆砌不仅占用空间,还诱发人的选择困难症,使人徒增烦恼;有的同学结合教师补充的资料解释了"极简主义"的概念并制作海报,呼吁实践低碳生活;还有同学录制了视频日志,利用公众号倡导健康积极的生活方式;还有同学决定尝试极简生活,处理掉不必要的生活物品,简化朋友圈,间歇性断网,将注意力转移到真正能够给人带来满足感和幸福感的事情上,比如读书、锻炼等。

在此案例分析的过程中,学生不但通过联系社会实际和自身经历,加深了对课文内容和作者观点的理解,而且融会贯通,学以致用,用创造性思维解决现实生活中的问题。

案例分析和讨论促使同学反思现有的生活方式,摒弃了物质至上、享乐主义的消费观,树立了积极向上的人生观和价值观。

三、课后任务

结合这一单元主题"财产占有对人的心理影响",教师布置了不同的小组项目任务,分别是人物访谈和问卷调查。

Do possessions make you happy?

采用项目教学法,通过这种微型的自主研究式学习,学生初步掌握科学研究的方法,了解基本的研究思路和逻辑,包括研究对象的选择、数据收集和分析等,为今后的学术研究打下基础。

通过问卷和访谈的"定量+定性"的实证研究,学生将文中所学观点在生活实际中加以检验,实现了文中所传递价值观的现实观照。对于与文中观点不一致的研究结果,学生则能阅读补充资料进行反思。

教学反思

本单元的主题是"财产占有对人的心理影响",作者从自身经历切入,阐述财产占有对人类心理的负面影响:自己买了一片小树林后,变得"沉重""贪婪""虚伪""自私"。首先,通过文本分析和对作者观点的解读,学生开始反思物质占有和幸福感之间的关系,并结合马斯洛的需求层级理论进一步思考何为自我实现的最高形式,什么才能带来持久的满足感。接下来,教师以"全球购物狂潮"为案例,引导学生分析消费主义的深层原因,从经济、环境、健康、文化等多个维度探讨消费主义的影响,反思自己的生活方式。此外,学生了解了极简主义和断舍离,摒弃对"买买买"和物质占有的痴迷,转而追求可持续、积极健康的生活方式,实现精神上的富足。

4. Educational Interpreting: Ceremonial Speeches

课程名称：口译理论与实践
教学对象：英语专业三年级学生
学时安排：1学时
教学目标： ✓ 知识目标：掌握致辞的惯用英语表达 　　　　　　了解口译训练技巧 ✓ 技能目标：运用口译笔记原则，分析和评价自己和同伴的笔记 　　　　　　运用箭头符号和缩略语完成口译笔记 ✓ 情感目标：从知名校长的演讲中培养放眼世界的胸怀 　　　　　　提升学习口译笔记的兴趣
教学重点： 分析、评价自己和同伴的口译笔记
教学难点： 运用箭头符号和缩略语完成中等难度篇章的口译笔记

教学过程	设计说明
一、课前翻转 在学习通平台完成以下学习任务。 1. 观看视频 *Annual Address of Vice Chancellor of Cambridge University*，上传口译录音和口译笔记。 2. 重点词汇。 • pervasive 遍布的 • preponderantly 占优势地 • collegiate 大学的 • be committed to 致力于 • assertion 主张 • be consonant with 与……一致的 3. 背景知识。 • Annual Address of the Vice Chancellor	课前，通过**在线学习平台上传课前翻转的学习任务单**，包括重点词汇、相关视频的背景介绍、音频、视频等材料。学生按要求完成口译并进行全程录音。同时，上传口译笔记。 课前口译翻转能让教师提前了解学生对该口译视频材料的掌握程度和在口译中出现的共性问题，便于在线下教学中进行有针对性的答疑解惑。

• In her annual address, the vice chancellor of Cambridge University, Professor Alison Richard called on the University to continue championing the enduring value of **academic excellence**, while focusing on the importance of **institutional diversity**. Cambridge University is home to over 23,000 students from more than 140 countries. The **Collegiate Cambridge** is bound together by a deep-rooted sense of community and shared purpose. **二、课中口译知识点讲解** **（一）学生作业情况分析** **Students' scores**： Highest score：91 Average score：80.6 Lowest score：66 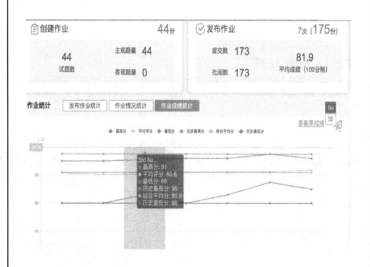 **（二）学生共性问题** **Some common problems**： 1. The University of Cambridge is a place, a community and an institution. institution 翻译成"机构"是否恰当？ 2. It is also a pervasive presence in the world. pervasive 翻译成"普遍存在"吗？ 3. That assertion is fully consonant with the … assertion 翻译成"假设"吗？	线下的授课主要分成两大模块：一是口译知识点的讲解，二是口译技巧的讲解。 **关于学生共性问题的讲解是翻转课堂的核心**，通过前期对学生口译表现的掌握，了解学生口译的薄弱环节。讲解前，先安排学生进行自主讨论，尝试得出几种不同的译本。 教师抛出共性问题供学生进行分组讨论，激发学生的自主学习热情。

（三）句子口译

The University of Cambridge is a place, a community and an institution. It is also a pervasive presence in the world. The Cambridge University Community is preponderantly British. 75% of our academic staff are British, 85% of our undergraduates, and almost 50% of our postgraduates.

Collegiate Cambridge remains deeply committed to the education of outstanding British students. That assertion is fully consonant with the Cambridge fast becoming more international in many, many ways.

学生"开小火车"进行句子口译，教师在每位学生完成口译后，进行针对性点评。遇到难度较大的句子，教师鼓励学生进行互评。评价基于"3C（clear, correct, coherent）"原则。

在进行句子口译时，遵循先集体复述再进行口译的原则。由于学生语言能力的差异，在学期前1/3的课程授课中会采取"源语复述＋目的语口译"的方式，缓解学生现场口译的压力。在进行后2/3的课程授课时，采用直接目的语口译的方式。

（四）教师分析口译要点

1. The University of Cambridge is a place, a community and an institution.

误译：剑桥大学是一个地方、一个社团、一个机构。

分析：这里的 community 可以翻译成"社区"。institution 不建议翻译成"机构"，可译为"研究机构"（research institution）。

2. It is also a pervasive presence in the world.

误译：这里也是世界普遍存在的。

分析：pervasive presence 不要翻译成"普遍存在"，否则译文会变成"剑桥大学是广泛存在的"，意思就错误了，可以意译为"具有广泛影响力"。

3. Community is preponderantly British. 75% of our academic staff are British, 85% of our undergraduates, and almost 50% of our postgraduates.

误译：这里英国学生的数量是占大多数的。75%的管理人员是英国人，85%的本科生还有几乎50%的研究生都是英国人。

分析：academic staff 建议翻译成"教学人员"或"学术人员"。

在口译要点分析环节，教师可以从学生的共性问题入手，结合之前讲授的口笔译技巧进行。例如，很多同学拘泥于单词的含义，例如 pervasive 只知其意为"普遍的、遍布的"，无法进行灵活转化。因此，在课后辅导中，教师会根据学生的实际口译水平，通过在线题库推送相关口译练习。

4. Collegiate Cambridge remains deeply committed to the education of outstanding British students.

学生译:剑桥大学仍然致力于让英国学生接受杰出的教育。

老师译:剑桥大学仍然致力培养杰出的英国学生。

5. That assertion is fully consonant with the Cambridge fast becoming more international in many, many ways.

误译:那一主张让剑桥大学未来迅速走向国际化。

分析:部分同学最后一个句子中"be consonant with"以及"in many, many ways"来不及记录,导致误译。

三、课中口译技巧教学

1. 小组活动:学生在线填写口译中遇到的困难。

2. 在线答题:为什么需要口译笔记?

通过在线学习中心,学生在线答题,教师可直接了解学生对口译技巧的掌握情况。例如,这节课就设计了"口译笔记重要性"的在线答题,了解学生们对口译笔记作用的认识。

从学生的答题中，教师总结出口译笔记的三大作用：一是帮助记录重要信息；二是有助于译员进行逻辑分析；三是减轻记忆负荷。

3. 小组讨论：口译笔记学生互评。
(1) 口译笔记评价维度。
- 口译笔记的排列（Arrangement of the notes）
- 合理使用箭头、缩略语和特殊符号（Proper use of arrows, abbreviations and symbols）
- 可识别（Readable）
- 有逻辑（Logic）

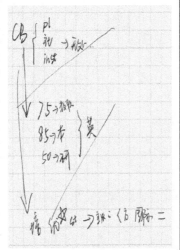

(2) 学生笔记优势分析。
- 句子之间的分割线（Separation of the sentences）
- 表示逻辑的箭头使用（Usage of arrows）

(3) 学生口译笔记建议。
- 不必写下完整的单词（Do not write down the whole words.）
- 可更多使用符号和缩略语（Better use more symbols and abbreviations.）

　　该生口译笔记逻辑性较强，能清晰地进行意群的划分。同时，对于重要信息的记录都比较完整。从她的记录中，可以看到她能非常熟练地运用箭头符号表示各类逻辑关系。因此，结合同学们的生生互评，建议该生在记录的时候可以再精简一些，例如，不需要完整记录"国际"这个词。

相关内容参见胡雅楠《口译笔记实战指导》中的第一章《口译笔记的重要性》。

在课堂授课中，学生的生生互评尤为关键。此处教学设计中体现了学生结合所学到的口译笔记评价标准，对某个同学的口译笔记进行现场点评。学生不仅需要点评该生的优点，还需要给出至少 1 个建议。

在这节课上，教师结合学生给出的各类笔记建议，梳理了该生口译笔记的优势和可进步的空间。需要强调的是，口译笔记极具个人特色，因此建议从逻辑性、笔记的结构等方面结合其口译表现综合给出建议。

（4）口译笔记技巧梳理。
• 纵向排列(Vertical arrangement)
• 意群分割(Separation of the sense group)
• 使用箭头、特殊符号及缩写(Proper use of arrows, symbols and abbreviation)
 	
（5）常用笔记符号复习。
 	
➤ 符号
    □   country
    :   say, speak
    ?   question, issue
    ☆   important, best, outstanding
    !   danger, warning
    &   relationship
    ×   wrong, mistake, bad
    √   good, correct
    =   the same as, equal to
    >   more than, exceed, surpass
    <   less than, inferior to
    +   plus, add, besides
    −   minus, deduct
 	
➤ 箭头
    ↑   rise, go up, increase, grow, expand, develop
    ↓   decrease, drop, go down, descend
    →   lead to, export to
    ←   come from, originate from, import from
 	
➤ 缩写
    JV: joint venture
    R&D: research and development
    FDI: foreign direct investment
    EU: European Union
    APEC: Asia-Pacific Economic Cooperation
    CIIE: China International Import Expo
	在本节课的口译笔记讲解中，教师和学生一起梳理了口译笔记技巧。同时，再次复习了前期的口译笔记常用符号。这些符号能帮助学生搭建属于自己的口译笔记系统。

四、课后作业布置

1. 第三组同学将 Simulation 3(情景口译对话 3)上传至课程中心,第四组准备 Simulation 4(情景口译对话 4),期末整个班完成一份《情景口译对话集锦》。
2. 视译 P.58 Section 1 课文。
3. 听译视频,将口译笔记和口译录音上传至"在线学习中心"。
4. 预习 Unit 5 Section 2 Vocabulary。
5. 学生根据学期初制订的"每周学习计划",自主完成口译题库中的练习题。

> 每次的课后作业都是为了下节课更好地进行翻转。在平时作业加分项中,**每位同学根据自己的实际情况,自主制订额外的课外练习计划**。期初交计划,期末交最终完成情况。与此同时,教师安排一对一的口译课后工作坊来监督学生的完成情况。

序号	事项	说明	预期分值	计划/实际	10周学习计划									
					第二周	第三周	第四周	第五周	第六周	第七周	第八周	第九周	第十周	第十一周
1	每周完成1篇 dictation	完成后上传至在线学习中心 dictation 栏目,每篇0.1分,满分1分		计划										
				实际										
2	每周完成1篇额外的口译练习	完成后上传至在线学习中心每周口译栏目,每篇0.1分,满分1分		计划										
				实际										
3	完成对其他小组的口译点评	点评1组0.1分,按实际点评小组数量计算		计划										
				实际										
4	每周完成题库中的句子翻译练习(显示"难"完成1题;显示"中"的完成2题;显示"易"完成3题)	每周完成得0.1分,满分1分		计划										
				实际										
5	参加1次口译课后辅导 workshop,并上传1次辅导反思	参加并上传反思得1分		计划										
				实际										
6	参加笔译、口译证书考试	参加(不论通过与否)得1分;通过得3分		计划										
				实际										
7	参加笔译、口译比赛	参加(不论通过与否)得1分;比赛获奖者得3分		计划										
				实际										
8	参加课外口译实践活动	参加老师认可的各类口译实践活动,1次1分;上限3分		计划										
				实际										

说明:期末递交最终的完成情况表和佐证电子材料(例如在线学习中心的截图、参加笔译、口译证书考试或比赛的证明、参加口译实践活动的照片等)

(平时作业加分项)

板书设计

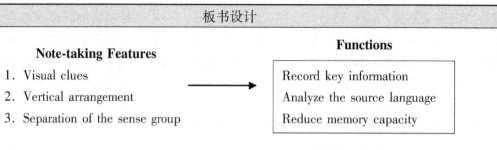

教学反思

"口译理论与实践"是英语专业大三的一门必修课,口译能力是英语专业本科生应具备的重要基本功之一。从前几届学生的课程反馈来看,口译课程对学生而言,难度较大,很多同学在上口译课的第一天就有畏难情绪。

首先,教师针对同学们普遍反映的问题,调整了教学目标,这门课程的目标侧重于培养学生的汉英双语表达及互译能力,提升他们的口译技巧(包括记笔记能力、顺译技巧和快速反应能力)。

其次,在整个授课过程中参考了布雷茨曼(Bretzmann)提出的"翻转课堂 2.0 阶段"及混合式教学课程范式,旨在让学生通过口译视频内容和口译技巧翻转的教学方式来理解口译技巧,从而提升口译听辨能力。

本节课的主题是教育系列口译,本次授课主要有三个教学环节:第一环节是课前翻转,进行译前主题准备和语言准备;第二环节是课中口译知识点讲解;第三环节是课中口译技巧教学,本章节着重培养的是口译笔记能力。

第一环节课前翻转是译前准备。刘和平教授在《口译技巧——思维科学与口译推理教学法》一书中指出,口译前教师要根据学生的语言水平和认知水平为他们提前扫清语言点障碍。近几年,学生英语水平差异性很大,如果课上直接进行口译,很多情况下会变成另一种形式的听力课。因此,教师采用了翻转课堂的模式,提前将口译材料、相关背景和语言知识点提供给学生,让他们课前上传自己口译的录音和口译笔记。这样,课中教师可以花更多时间在他们口译的共性问题上。同时,根据学生的口译问题,教师再及时调整口译练习的难度,将宝贵的课堂时间变成学生讨论及评价各自口译的机会。

第二环节课中口译知识点讲解是口译视频的翻转,本节课选取的是剑桥大学校长的年度致辞。对于学生而言,世界知名大学校长的演讲能激发他们继续深造的动力。在这个部分,教师把教学重点放在同学们的共性问题上,比如,同学们普遍不知道 pervasive 这个单词如何翻译。教师在课上就可以根据他们的问题,进行有针对性的解答。此外,学生对数字口译不熟悉,例如,本次口译视频出现了 3 个数字(75% 的教学人员、85% 的本科生和近 50% 的研究生),这些数字到底代表什么?教师也需要在课上特别强调。

第三环节着重于口译技巧的翻转。学生在线讨论"为什么需要口译笔记",可畅所欲言,大家普遍认为,口译笔记可以帮助减轻认知负荷,提供主要的信息,建立口译者的信心。同时,教师让学生自己总结口译笔记的记录原则。首先要纵向排列,其次是意群的分割,最后就是正确使用箭头、特殊符号及缩略语。

例如,在本次视频口译笔记中,使用方框表示"国家",小星星表示"重要"。在经典的巴黎高翻释意理论中,强调记录要"脱去源语语言外壳",要进入语言的"意义层面",因此,可将口译笔记也理解为摆脱文字本身的束缚,用符号和关键词记录的带有逻辑意义的文本。所以,教师会告诉学生在笔记学习中,一定要将符号系统化,要抵住将字记全的冲动,只需要记录关键的缩略语即可。

在课后作业布置环节,教师进行了下一节课的翻转,布置了预习、口译分组及下一节课的课前练习。教师给学生展示前几届学生的口译笔记,鼓励他们继续努力。一个学期的口译学习并不能很好地解决学生的听记协调问题。因此,在后续的课程设计上,教师会继续总结学生的口译问题,在题库中根据学生的薄弱点进行更具针对性的练习推送。

第二章

"综合英语"教学设计

1. Book 4 Unit 1 Never Give In, Never, Never, Never (1)

课程名称	综合英语	学时安排	1 学时
教学对象	英语专业二年级学生		
教学目标	The students will be able to: 1. brush up on their background knowledge of Winston Churchill; 2. figure out the structure of the text; 3. identify basic rhetorical features of a speech.		
教学思想	1. Improve the students' ability of close reading. 2. Construct a teaching cycle from input to output, encouraging collaborative and autonomous learning. 3. Strengthen the students' language skills, humanistic quality and critical thinking literacy.		
教学分析			
教学内容	Background information, structural analysis, rhetorical analysis		
教学重点	Background information, structural analysis, rhetorical analysis		
教学难点	Rhetorical analysis		
教学方法	1. Close reading 2. Collaborative learning		
教学过程			
课堂教学安排	➢ 本次课程内容介绍: 　　本次课是演讲文的第一次课,主要用以介绍温斯顿·丘吉尔的背景知识,并对全文做结构分析和修辞分析。 ➢ 以下为本节课的具体步骤: Part Ⅰ: Preview Task Part Ⅱ: Lead-in Part Ⅲ: Structural Analysis Part Ⅳ: Rhetorical Analysis Part Ⅴ: Assignment		

I. Preview Task

☐ Read the supplementary materials about Winston Churchill written by John Keegan before class.（课前通过课程中心发布文章）

☐ Draw a map of his political life.

II. Lead-in

Q1: What do you know about Winston Churchill?

1. Find out all the jobs done by Winston Churchill.
2. Why was he determined to enter the political field?
3. Comment on his political life before WW II.
4. Comment on his political life during WW II.
5. What happened to him after WW II?

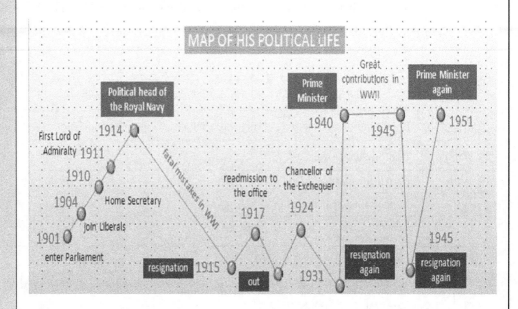

Task for students: Use the map to retell Winston Churchill's life.

Q2: What is the feature of his political life?

☐ Ups and downs.

☐ Never give in, never, never, never!!!

III. Structural Analysis

This text is an inspiring speech made by Winston Churchill, Great Britain's then Prime Minister, when he visited Harrow School on 29 October, 1941. The whole speech can be divided into three parts.

Part I (Para.1)	Opening remarks	Churchill summarized __what had happened__ since his last visit to Harrow.
Part II (Paras.2—5)	The body	Churchill drew the __lessons__ to be learned from the past year.
Part III (Paras.6—8)	The conclusion	Churchill, by __changing a word__ in the school song, expressed his conviction that the entire nation was blessed with the chance to display its courage to the full.

IV. Rhetorical Analysis

Q: What are the rhetorical features of a speech?

Example 1   Obama's victory speech

As Lincoln said to a nation far more divided than ours, "We are not enemies, but friends ... though passion may have strained, it must not break our bonds of affection." and to those Americans whose support I have yet to earn—I may not have won your vote tonight, but I hear your voices, I need your help, and I will be your President too.

Examples from the text

... and as Kipling well says, we must "... meet with Triumph and Disaster. And treat those two impostors just the same."

Example 2   Obama's victory speech

At a time when women's voices were silenced and their hopes dismissed, she lived to see them stand up and speak out and reach for the ballot. Yes we can. When there was despair in the dust bowl and depression across the land, she saw a nation conquer fear itself with a new deal, new jobs and a new sense of common purpose. Yes we can. When the bombs fell on our harbor and tyranny threatened the world, she was there to witness a generation rise to greatness and a democracy was saved. Yes we can.

Examples from the text

But for everyone, surely, what we have gone through in this period—I am addressing myself to the school—surely from this period of ten months this is the lesson: **Never give in, never give in, never, never, never, never**—in nothing, great or small, large or petty—never give in except to convictions of honor and good sense.

Example 3 Hilary's concession speech

I want to start today by saying how grateful I am to all of you, to everyone **who poured your hearts and your hopes into this campaign, who drove for miles and lined the streets waving homemade signs, who scrimped and saved to raise money, who knocked on doors and made calls, who talked, sometimes argued with your friends and neighbors, who e-mailed and contributed online, who invested so much in our common enterprise**, to the moms and dads who came to **our events, who lifted their little girls and little boys on their shoulders** and whispered in their ears, "See, you can be anything you want to be."

Examples from the text

It is generally said that the British are often better at the last. They do not expect to move from crisis to crisis; they don't always expect that each day will bring up some noble chance of war.

Quotation
Repetition } Add power and strength to the speech effectively.
Parallelism

V. Assignment

1. Watch the video clip from *Into the Storm* and get to know more about Winston Churchill.

   ☐ What consequence would it be if the German took over the French navy?
   ☐ What was Churchill's plan if French did not accept his choices? Why would he do so?

2. Read the text carefully and try to find some other important *rhetoric* used by the author.

附1:本节重点词汇
repetition, parallelism, alliteration, quotation

附2:补充资料
◇ 通过网络课程中心发布,由学生课后下载并完成。
1. *Winston Churchill* written by John Keegan
2. *Into the Storm*(video)

教学反思

　　本节课是主课文的第一次授课,预习环节中的绘图任务充分调动了学生的预习兴趣,并有效支撑了课堂教学的顺利进行。

　　导入阶段的思维图谱帮助学生较好地完成了复述任务,也让他们对写作的时代背景有所了解。

　　在结构分析环节,大部分学生能提炼出各个部分的关键词,从而形成对篇章结构的整体认识。

　　修辞分析环节架起了课文与经典演说的关联,帮助学生掌握了三种重要修辞手段及其修辞意义,从而理解演说这一题材的基本范式。

2. Book 4 Unit 1 Never Give In, Never, Never, Never (2)

课程名称	综合英语	学时安排	1学时
教学对象	英语专业二年级学生		
教学目标	The students will be able to: 1. learn the vocabulary and grammar; 2. learn how to guess the meaning of new expressions.		
教学思想	1. Improve the students' ability of close reading. 2. Construct a teaching cycle from input to output, encouraging collaborative and autonomous learning. 3. Strengthen the students' language skills, humanistic quality and critical thinking literacy.		
教学分析			
教学内容	Vocabulary; detailed reading (Paras. 3 – 4); guess the meaning of new expressions		
教学重点	Detailed reading (Paras. 3 – 4), guess the meaning of new expressions		
教学难点	Guess the meaning of new expressions		
教学方法	1. Close reading 2. Collaborative learning		
教学过程			
课堂教学安排	➢ 本次课程内容介绍： 　　本次课是这篇演讲文的第三课，前两次课已经介绍了本文的体裁特点和结构，分析了第1—2段的文章内容。本次课将分析第3—4段。 ➢ 以下为本节课的具体步骤： Part Ⅰ: Brief Review Part Ⅱ: Detailed Reading (Paras. 3 – 4) Part Ⅲ: Assignment		

Ⅰ. Brief Review

Part 1 (Para. 1)

Catastrophic events
Ups and downs } The world situation in the past ten months
Misfortunes

Ten months ago	Now
Quite alone, desperately alone	
Poorly armed	Improved
Air attack	

→ Thankful but impatient

Part 2 { (Para. 2) (Para. 3) (Para. 4) }   Lesson 1: learn to be equally good at what is short and sharp and what is long and tough

Ⅱ. Detailed Reading (Paras. 3 – 4)

Para. 3: Another lesson I think we may take, just throwing our minds back to our meeting here ten months ago and now, is that appearances are often very deceptive, and as Kipling well says, we must "... meet with Triumph and Disaster. And treat those two imposters just the same."

Q1: What's the second lesson?

重点句: Appearances are often deceptive.

deceptive: *a.* misleading

Derivation: deception *n.*
              deceive *v.*

Paraphrase: Surface phenomena are often misleading.

Q2: Do you agree?

Q3: Why did Churchill quote Kipling as saying "treat those two imposters just the same"?

课堂教学安排

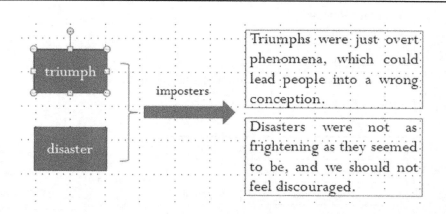

Para. 4: You can't tell from appearances how things will go. Sometimes imagination makes things out far worse than they are; yet without imagination not much can be done. Those people who are imaginative see many more dangers than perhaps exist; certainly many more will happen; but then they must also pray to be given that extra courage to carry this far-reaching imagination. But for everyone, surely, what we have gone through in this period—I am addressing myself to the school—surely from this period of ten months this is the lesson: never give in, never give in, never, never, never, never—in nothing, great or small, large or petty—never give in except to convictions of honor and good sense. Never yield to force; never yield to the apparently overwhelming might of the enemy. We stood all alone a year ago, and to many countries it seemed that our account was closed, we were finished. All this tradition of ours, our songs, our school history, this part of the history of this country, were gone and finished and liquidated.

Q4: What's the role of imagination?
Language point:
imagination, imaginative, imaginable, imaginary, imagine
It's _____ that _____ is very important for an artist and he/she has to be _____ in order to create vivid _____ works of art. Can you _____ an artist who lacks _____ ?

Advantages	Disadvantages
Without it, not much can be done.	It makes things out far worse than they are.
People who are imaginative see many more dangers than perhaps exist.	They must also pray to be given that extra courage to carry out this far-reaching imagination.

Q5: What's the third lesson?

Never give in, never give in, never, never, never, never—in nothing, great or small, large or petty—never give in except to convictions of honor and good sense.

Rhetorical analysis $\begin{cases} \text{repetition} \\ \text{use of antonyms} \end{cases}$ ⟹ To emphasize "under no circumstance should we give in"

重点句: Our account was closed.

How to guess the meaning of new expressions?
1. Association.

At the bank: open an account < - - > close an account ⟹ The banking business is over.

Metaphorically: The country is over.

2. Context.

We were finished. All this tradition of ours, our songs, our school history, this part of the history of this country, <u>were gone and finished and liquidated</u>.

由上下文判断: The country is over.

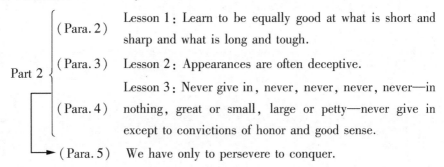

Lesson 1: Learn to be equally good at what is short and sharp and what is long and tough. (Para. 2)

Lesson 2: Appearances are often deceptive. (Para. 3)

Lesson 3: Never give in, never, never, never, never—in nothing, great or small, large or petty—never give in except to convictions of honor and good sense. (Para. 4)

(Para. 5) We have only to persevere to conquer.

III. Assignment

➢ Read the speech—"Blood, toil, tears and sweat" made by Churchill in 1940 when he took the oath as the Prime Minister.

➢ Compare and contrast this speech with the speech we learned in the text.

附1:本节重点词汇
deceptive, imagination, imaginative, imaginary, imaginable, imposter

附2:补充资料
通过网络课程中心发布,由学生课后下载并完成。
Supplementary reading: "Blood, toil, tears and sweat"

教学反思

  本节课主要是对课文的精读分析,在实际授课中发现,学生普遍对丘吉尔引用的名言理解不够深刻,同时对 imagination 的负面作用的理解不够到位。通过启发式提问,学生基本能厘清丘吉尔第二条经验的逻辑思路。

3. Book 2 Unit 7 The Jeaning of America

课程名称	综合英语	学时安排	1学时
教学对象	英语专业一年级学生		
教学目标	The students will be able to: 1. retell the history of jeans; 2. identify writing techniques employed in the first paragraph; 3. introduce the symbol of Chinese culture.		
教学思想	1. Improve the students' genre awareness of different text types. 2. Construct a teaching cycle from input to output, encouraging collaborative and autonomous learning. 3. Strengthen the students' language skills, humanistic quality and critical thinking literacy.		
教学分析			
教学内容	Lead-in; generic features and structure; writing techniques		
教学重点	Generic features of exposition and the structure		
教学难点	Writing techniques		
教学方法	1. Genre-based teaching 2. Collaborative learning		
教学过程			
课堂教学安排	➢ 本次课程内容介绍: 　　第一学期已经讨论过说明文常见的体裁特征。本单元的说明文与之前不同,主体部分有较多的记叙文元素,但仍属于说明文的范畴,因为文章并非Levi的传记,而是牛仔裤的发展历程。因此,本单元将着重引导学生关注时间线索,找到牛仔裤发展历程中的重要阶段,从而学会复述,并能利用文章中所学的写作技巧完成仿写的语言输出任务。 ➢ 以下为本节课的具体步骤: Part Ⅰ: Lead-in Part Ⅱ: Generic Structure Part Ⅲ: Global Reading Part Ⅳ: Discussion Part Ⅴ: Detailed Reading of Para. 1 Part Ⅵ: Mini-Presentation Part Ⅶ: Assignment		

I. Lead-in

Video watching——*Blue Jeans*

Video 1:

Q1: What emotions/messages are conveyed in this video?

Answer: Enthusiasm, equality, comfort, relax, energy.

Video 2:

Q2: What happened in 1873?

Answer: The government gave Strauss and Davis a patent for their invention of rivets.

Q3: What American values do jeans represent?

Answer: Creativity and rebellion.

II. Generic Structure

Compare and contrast the structure of Unit 5 with that of Unit 7.

Answer: The difference lies in the body part, mainly Paras. 2–6 in this text. The main body of this unit is not organized by topic sentences and supporting details, but by chronological order. Different time markers indicate different stages of the history of the jeans. It looks like a biography, but the focus is not on Levi, but on the jeans.

III. Global Reading

Use Para. 3 as an example to show students how to grasp the general picture and retell.

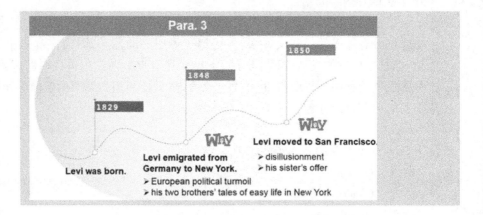

Q1: Why did Levi emigrate from Germany to New York?

Q2: Why did Levi move from New York to San Francisco in 1950?

IV. Discussion

Work in groups and use the storyline map to retell Paras. 4 – 6.

Paragraph	Task 1: Information	Task 2: Comprehension	Task 3: Retelling
4	1	1	1
5	2	2	2
6	3	3	3

V. Detailed Reading of Para. 1

The Jeaning of America

Carin Quinn

This is the story of a sturdy American symbol which has now spread throughout most of the world. The symbol is not the dollar. It is not even Coca-Cola. It is a simple pair of pants called blue jeans, and what the pants symbolize is what Alexis de Tocqueville called "a manly and legitimate passion for equality …" Blue jeans are favored equally by bureaucrats and cowboys, bankers and deadbeats, fashion designers and beer drinkers. They draw no distinctions and recognize no classes: They are merely American. Yet they are sought after almost everywhere in the world—including Russia, where authorities recently broke up a teenaged gang that was selling them on the black market for two hundred dollars a pair. They have been around for a long time. And it seems likely that they will outlive even the necktie.

The Title:

Jeaning: A gerund indicating a process or development. Therefore, the title means the development or history of the jeans of America.

Para. 1

Q: How does the author prove that blue jeans stand for "a passion for equality"? (Para. 1)

A: The author mentions that the pants draw no distinction and recognize no classes. They are favored by people from all walks of life, whether they are cowboys or bureaucrats.

课堂教学安排

1. Words and expressions.
- **symbol** *n*. something that represents an idea

e.g. It was a mysterious place, a symbol of the unreachable and the remote.
The lion is the symbol of courage.

Derivation:

symbolic *a*.

symbolism *n*.

symbolize *v*.

Synonym:

representation

Collocation:

symbol of　something that represents or suggests something else, such as an idea or quality

e.g. In the picture the tree is the symbol of life and the snake is the symbol of evil.

symbol for　a letter, sign, or figure which expresses a sound, operation, number, chemical substance, etc.

e.g. On maps, a cross is the symbol for a church.

- **legitimate** *a*. able to be defended with logic or justification; legally valid

e.g. The Crown Prince has a legitimate claim to the throne. I'm not sure that his business is strictly legitimate.

Derivation:

legitimately *ad*.

legitimacy *n*.

Antonym:

illegitimate

- **favor** *n*. an act of gracious kindness; an advantage to the benefit of someone or something

e.g. He did all he could do to win her favor.
I'm sure the president will look with favor on such a proposal.

v. to promote over another; to consider as the favorite

e.g. Among his three daughters, he favors the second one.
The local football team was favored by the spectators from different areas.

<table>
<tr><td rowspan="2">课
堂
教
学
安
排</td><td>

Derivation: favorable *a*.

Collocation: be in/out of one's favor; in favor of sb./sth.

- **seek** *vt.* to try to find or obtain

e.g. seek refuge/asylum

　　seek revenge/compensation

2. Summary of writing techniques.

Exemplification; comparison and contrast; quotation.

VI. Mini-Presentation

Introduce one symbol of China—the dragon by using the above techniques.

VII. Assignment

Write a paragraph of no less than 150 words to introduce your idea of the symbol of China by using the author's writing techniques.

</td></tr>
</table>

教学反思

　　本节课的教学主要以学生展示的形式进行，主题为中国文化象征，这对学生来说是个挑战。为了确保任务的顺利完成，教师将此输出任务分为课前、课中和课后三大板块。学生在课前需要完成中国文化的象征——龙的相关学习，包括视频及线上讨论。课中对第一段的写作手法的分析帮助学生掌握介绍中国文化象征的基本方法，通过示范让学生明白技巧具体运用的场景，学生接下来的展示也就水到渠成。从课堂表现来看，由于学生准备充分，整个活动环节达到了既定效果，加深了学生对中国文化的了解，也使得学生能利用课堂所学完成语言输出任务。课后作业是这一语言输出任务的深化，学生需要综合运用三种写作技巧完成对中国文化的介绍。由于课前和课中讨论已经对此任务做了足够的铺垫，这一输出任务实际完成情况良好。

4. Book 4 Unit 6 The Discus Thrower（1）

课程名称	综合英语	学时安排	1学时
教学对象	英语专业二年级学生		
教学目标	The students will be able to： 1. learn the vocabulary and grammar in Paras. 1–3； 2. understand rules for effective observation.		
教学思想	1. Improve the students' ability for close reading. 2. Construct a teaching cycle from input to output, encouraging collaborative and autonomous learning. 3. Strengthen the students' language skills, humanistic quality and critical thinking literacy.		
教学分析			
教学内容	Introduction to the author, Paras. 1–3, effective observation		
教学重点	Paras. 1–3, effective observation		
教学难点	Paras. 1–3, effective observation		
教学方法	1. Humanistic close reading 2. Collaborative learning		
教学策略	1. Use multimedia resources to facilitate teaching and learning 2. Activate students' language, grammar and culture scheme through different tasks		
教学过程			
课堂教学安排	➢ 本次课程内容介绍： 　　本文为描写文，以病入膏肓的绝望的病人为观察着眼点，细致描述了病房环境和病人每日扔盘子的举动。本次课为第一、二、三段内容的精读。 ➢ 以下为本节课的具体步骤： Part Ⅰ：Lead-in：Introduction to the Author Part Ⅱ：Exploring the Content（Paras. 1–3） Part Ⅲ：Exploring the Strategy Part Ⅳ：Assignment		

I. Lead-in: Introduction to the Author

As a writer: humanistic and emotional

As a surgeon: professional, with penetrating view

II. Exploring the Content (Paras. 1–3)

Para. 1: I spy on my patients. Ought not a doctor to observe his patients by any means and from any stance, that he might all the more fully assemble the evidence? So I stand in the doorways of hospital rooms and gaze. Oh, it is not all that furtive an act. Those in bed need only look up to discover me. But they never do.

Q1: What does "spy on" mean?

A: Taking a furtive look at.

辨析: spy on, peer, peep, pry into

1. Blake screwed up his eyes, trying to _____ through the fog.
2. Jerry _____ through the keyhole into the kitchen.
3. I'm sick of you _____ my personal life.
4. The couple were _____ by FBI.

Q2: Find out the reasons given by the author that justify his furtive action of spying on his patients.

重点句1: Ought not a doctor to observe his patients by any means and from any stance, that he might all the more fully assemble the evidence?

1. Words and expressions.
   - **stance**: perspective
   - **all the more fully**: (all) + the + comparative degree of ad./a.
   - e.g. I know there is a danger for it, but I am all the more determined on driving forward.
   - **assemble**: to collect

Q3: What's the purpose of collecting evidence?

2. Translate the sentence into Chinese.

A: 医生难道不该采取任何手段,从任何位置观察病人,以便获得更加完整的证据吗?

3. Change the question into a statement.

A: A doctor ought to observe his patients by any means and from any stance so that he might all the more fully assemble the evidence.

Q4: What's the figure of speech?

A: Rhetorical question.

Q5: What's the function of this rhetorical question?

A: To emphasize that he's totally justified to spy on his patients.

重点句 2: Those in bed need only look up in order to discover me. But they never do.

Q6: Why would they never do?

A: Because these terminally ill patients know their days are numbered. They have already lost hope in living.

Para. 2: From the doorway of Room 542, the man in the bed seems deeply tanned. Blue eyes and close-cropped white hair give him the appearance of vigor and good health. But I know that his skin is not brown from the sun. It is rusted, rather, in the last stage of containing the vile repose within. And the blue eyes are frosted, looking inward like the windows of a snowbound cottage. This man is blind. This man is also legless—the right leg missing from midthigh down, the left from just below the knee. It gives him the look of a bonsai, roots and branches pruned into the dwarfed facsimile of a great tree.

1. Task for students: Underline words or phrases used to describe his physical condition (Para. 2).

skin	deeply-tanned; _____
eyes	blue; blind; _____
hair	white; _____
body	legless; _____

2. Words and expressions.

deeply tanned

rusted

vile repose

- **vile** *a.* extremely unpleasant
- **repose** *n.* temporary rest from activity, excitement, or exertion, especially sleep or the rest given by sleep

Note: allusion

Lord Byron's poem "The Prisoner of Chillon"(《西雍的囚徒》)

3. Task for students: Read the poem and find out what "vile repose" means to the prisoner in this poem.

frosted, looking inward like the windows of a snowbound cottage

-bound: fog-bound, wheelchair-bound

e. g. The serious traffic accident on the fog-bound expressway left him wheelchair-bound for his remaining days.

小组讨论1

Q7: What can you see from the description of the physical appearance of the patient?

Q8: Why does the author compare him to a bonsai?

Para. 3: The room in which he dwells is empty of all possessions—no get-well cards, small, private caches of food, day-old flowers, slippers, all the usual kickshaws of the sickroom. There is only the bed, a chair, a nightstand, and a tray on wheels that can be swung across his lap for meals.

小组讨论2

Q9: Find out the unusualness of the patient's room.

Q10: What can you see from the description of his room?

课堂教学安排	**III. Exploring the Strategy** Rule 1: Use images that are closely related to your purpose. Rule 2: Use contrast. Rule 3: Show rather than tell. Simile　明喻 Metaphor　暗喻 Allusion　借用典故 **IV. Assignment** 1. Expand the statement "I grew tired after dinner" into a vivid description within 150 words by using a variety of rhetorical devices. 2. Find out other techniques that are employed by the author to produce effective observation.

附1：本节重点词汇

spy on, furtive, peer, peep, pry into, stance, rhetorical question, all the more, deeply-tanned, rusted, vile repose, -bound, allusion, metaphor, simile

附2：补充资料 Lord Byron's poem "The Prisoner of Chillon"

通过网络课程中心发布，由学生课后下载并完成。

教学反思

　　本次教学的重难点有三个方面：其一是关于叙述者对于病人的偷窥举动，教师以偷窥是否合理为线索，引导学生完成对第一段的分析，从而使学生了解病人的基本生存状态。其二是对扔盘子病人的外貌描写，叙述者在第二段以近景方式细致描绘了这位特殊病人的外貌。教师以搜寻关键词的形式，引导学生聚焦病人的肤色、眼睛、头发和身体等几大外貌特征，结合多种修辞手法的分析，探究外貌描写背后的深义。实际教学中，学生普遍认为典故引用理解难度较大。其三是病房的环境描写，通过分析病房的与众不同，引导学生关注环境描写在衬托人物形象上所起的重要作用。

5. Book 4 Unit 6 The Discus Thrower (2)

课程名称	综合英语	学时安排	1学时
教学对象	英语专业二年级学生		
教学目标	The students will be able to: 1. learn the vocabulary and grammar in Para. 5 and Para. 10; 2. understand pun and irony; 3. understand the theme of the text.		
教学思想	1. Improve the students' ability for close reading. 2. Construct a teaching cycle from input to output, encouraging collaborative and autonomous learning. 3. Strengthen the students' language skills, humanistic quality and critical thinking literacy.		
教学分析			
教学内容	Para. 5, Para. 10, pun, irony, theme		
教学重点	Para. 5, Para. 10, pun, irony, theme		
教学难点	Pun, irony, theme		
教学方法	1. Humanistic close reading 2. Collaborative learning		
教学策略	1. Use multimedia resources to facilitate teaching and learning. 2. Activate students' language, grammar and culture scheme through different tasks.		
教学过程			
课堂教学安排	➢ 本次课程内容介绍: 　　本文为描写文,以病入膏肓的绝望的病人为观察着眼点,细致描述了病房环境和病人每日扔盘子的举动。本次课为第5段和第10段内容的精读。 ➢ 以下为本节课的具体步骤: Part Ⅰ: Brief Review Part Ⅱ: Exploring the Content (Para. 5, Para. 10) Part Ⅲ: Exploring the Strategy Part Ⅳ: Exploring the Theme Part Ⅴ: Assignment		

I. Brief Review

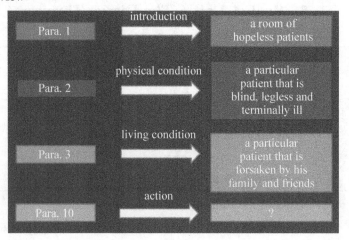

II. Exploring the Content (Para. 5, Para. 10)

Discussion: Why does the author choose the title "The Discus Thrower" for his story?

Para. 5:

Dialogue	Implied meaning
"What time is it?" he asks. "Three o'clock." "Morning or afternoon?" "Afternoon." He's silent. There is nothing else he wants to know.	He is blind. He is hopeless. There is nothing else he wants to know.
"How are you?" I say. "Who are you?" he asks.	No one has ever cared about him. The doctor's greeting shocks him. He's mistrustful.
"It's the doctor. How do you feel?" He doesn't answer right away. "Feel?" he says. "I hope you feel better," I say.	This shows he's numb in emotion. His plight throws him into despair and he has lost hope for anything, waiting for his final moment to come. He asks the question rhetorically, which indicates his annoyance. He thinks it's stupid for the doctor to ask how he feels given the present condition he is in.
I press the button at the side of the bed. "Down you go," I say. "Yes, down," he says.	What the doctor means is that the man's bed is being lowered, yet the patient takes it to mean that he's getting closer to death.

Para. 10:

In time the man reaches to find the rim of the tray, then on to find the dome of the covered dish. He lifts off the cover and places it on the stand. He fingers across the plate until he probes the eggs. He lifts the plate in both hands, sets it on the palm of his right hand, centers it, balances it. He hefts it up and down slightly, getting the feel on it. Abruptly, he draws back his right arm as far as he can.

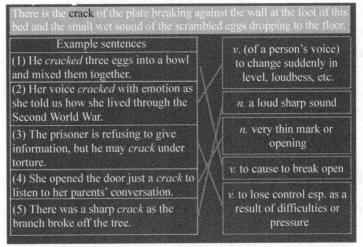

Task for students: Act out what's described in Para. 10.

III. Exploring the Strategy

➤ pun

e. g. Fitzgerald R. Ford (born in 1913, the 38th American President): "I am a Ford, not a Lincoln."

e. g. He drove his expensive car into a tree and found out how the Mercedes bends.

e. g. I used to be a banker but I lost interest.

Q1: How is irony created in the text?

➤ More examples of irony

Example #1
"The Gift of the Magi" by O. Henry

Example #2
"Today was a very cold and bitter day, as cold and bitter as a cup of hot chocolate, if the cup of hot chocolate had vinegar added to it and were placed in a refrigerator for several hours."

课堂教学安排	**IV. Exploring the Theme** Q2: Why does the patient throw the plate with scrambled eggs against the wall each day? **V. Assignment** 1. Find out more examples of irony in the text. 2. Explain how irony is created for each case. 3. Watch the video of Nick giving a speech. 4. How to face death? Draw a comparison and contrast between the man in the text and Nick. Write a short paragraph of reflection.

附1:本节重点词汇
pun, irony, crack, tray, stand, covered dish, theme
附2:补充资料
通过网络课程中心发布 the Video of Nick's Speech,由学生课后下载并完成。

教学反思

　　"为什么扔盘子?"是本单元学习的难点。为了充分引发学生的探究,讨论成为本节课的主要授课形式。因为有了前期细读的铺垫,大部分学生都能利用课文提供的细节展开有理有据的论述,并且能言之成理。

　　教师引入了尼克(Nick)的演说视频作为课堂学习的延伸,试图从另一个角度帮助学生看待死亡,尼克的态度与主人公的态度如何去评价,如何去理解,这些都值得学生深思。

第三章

"高级英语"教学设计

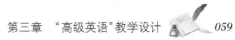

1. Book 6 Unit 1 A Class Act

课程名称	高级英语	教学对象	英语专业三年级学生
学时安排	4 学时		
教学目标	The students will be able to: 1. draft the plot diagram based on structural analysis; 2. detect the protagonist's characteristics and emotional change; 3. identify rhetorical devices; 4. appreciate the author's tone; 5. depict the characters' inner world.		
教学思想	1. Close reading based on textual evidence. 2. Collaborative and autonomous learning. 3. Integration of language skills, humanistic quality and critical thinking.		
教学分析			
教学内容	Lead-in, structural analysis, character analysis, writing strategies		
教学重点	Plot diagram, characterization, emotional change		
教学难点	Various rhetoric devices, the author's tone		
教学方法	Online discussion, lead-in video, Socratic questions, drafting diagram, peer review, electronic story		
教学过程			

<table>
<tr><td rowspan="2">课
堂
教
学
安
排</td><td>

I. Approaching the Topic

1. Lead-in activities.

- Online discussion: What makes a good teacher?
- Analyze the word cloud based on your responses and induce some dimensions that define a good teacher.
- Watch the video *How to Be a Good Teacher* and summarize some dos and don'ts in the video.
- You feel immensely warmed when hearing a nice word from teachers especially in times of frustration and depression. Share one such experience with the class.

2. Title interpretation.

Q1: What is the meaning of the title *A Class Act*?

Q2: How does the title function structurally and rhetorically?

</td></tr>
</table>

A: This is an informal phrase referring to someone who is admirable and usually very fair and polite. Here it refers to Miss McVee, the author's literature teacher. The author suggests that she was a first-class teacher.

Part 1

(Paras. 1 – 3) The author's family and their life during the war.

Part 2

(Paras. 4 – 7) The author's experience of humiliation in the school.

Part 3

(Paras. 8 – 11) How her excitement of a free photographic portrait sitting triggers her anticipation of the oncoming torment in the school.

Part 4

(Paras. 12 – 15) A turning point in the author's life.

Part 5

(Paras. 16 – 17) The immediate impact of a "warm sentence" by the teacher and its everlasting influence on the author.

II. Close Reading

1. Paras. 1 – 3.

◇ Q1: What does the author mean by "Yet I could not have asked for more enterprising and optimistic parents"?

A: My parents were the most enterprising and optimistic ones one could expect to find. The author thinks that her parents did all they could to support the family with their hard work, ingenuity and thrift, and that the family enjoyed "bucketloads of cheer".

◇ Q2: Why does the author still have some trouble in her school?

A: Because her parents were not able to buy the "blue blazer and hatband" required by the school.

Discussion:

— What is told about my parents?

— Is it direct or indirect characterization?

◇ Worksheet:

A: These three paragraphs give a brief description of the hard conditions during World War II, and how the author's parents managed to support the family and what they did for their children. Note that the last sentence of the third paragraph paves the way for the whole story.

rife *a.* very common and frequent

e. g. Dysentery and malaria are rife in the refugee camps.

   He leads a party in which corruption is rife.

2. Paras. 4 – 5.

◇ Q: How did the deputy headmistress teach the author a lesson?

A: The deputy headmistress made it her mission to teach the author a lesson for not complying with the school regulations. In the daily assembly she would pull her out of line and make her stand on the stage as a bad example.

comply *v.* to obey a rule or law, or to do what someone asks you to do

e. g. He's been ordered to have the dog destroyed because it's dangerous, but he refuses to comply.

The patient complied with the physician's orders.

3. Paras. 6 – 7.

Q1: What made the situation even worse for the author?

A: The situation was made even worse as the author was barred from the gym team and the weekly ballroom dancing class which she loved so much.

Q2: Why could the author not tell her mother about her humiliation in the school?

A: The author could not tell her mother about her humiliation because she did not want to run the risk of her mother coming to the school and being hurt by that unfeeling teacher. And if her mother told her father about it, he would have got very angry and even wanted to fight with the school authorities in order to protect her.

Discussion:

- Do you share similar experiences when there is suffering you would keep it only to yourself?
- Why is the exposition so lengthy? Is it necessary?

◇ Worksheet:

A: These two paragraphs describe how the author feels about this punishment—"battle back tears" "embarrassed" "desperately wished" "this horrid school" "ritual humiliation" "but to see the punishment through".

bar *vt.* to officially say that something must not happen, or that someone must not do something or go somewhere

e. g. He was barred from the contest.

A lack of formal education is no bar to becoming rich.

see … through: to continue doing something until it is finished, especially something unpleasant or difficult

e. g. He was a prisoner of war for five years, but his courage saw him through.

We'll see you through until you finish your college education.

I saw the project through and then resigned.

4. Paras. 8 – 9.

Q: How did the free portrait news make me feel? Why?

A: The free photographic portrait sitting stirred mixed feelings in the author. On the one hand, she was beside herself with excitement; on the other hand, she was aware of the upcoming torment she faced because of her dress (even though it was her best dress).

fuel *vt.* something that fuels a feeling or a type of behavior increases or strengthens it

e. g. The rapid promotion of the director's son has itself fuelled resentment within the company.

The chairman's speech fuelled speculation that he was about to resign.

5. Paras. 10 – 11.

Q1: Why did the author walk to the stage of her own accord?

A: Because her past experiences told her that such ritual punishment would occur anyway.

Q2: Why did the author feel so frustrated?

A: Because she simply could not understand why those unsympathetic teachers could not see that she was actually an obedient girl who was eager to participate in all the activities despite her clothes.

Discussion:

- Paraphrase Para. 11 in your own words.
- How does internal monologue contribute to characterization?

◇ Worksheet:

A: Pay attention to the words that reveal the author's feelings—"heavy-hearted" "dragged" "trudged". These two paragraphs describe what happens when the author goes to school in her green dress. She goes to the stage even without being requested to receive the routine humiliation and frustrating "sniggers of the other girls and the beady eyes of the deputy head"—and yearns to be understood.

drag *vt.* to pull something or someone along with difficulty; to make someone leave or go to a place when they do not want to do so

e. g. I really had to drag myself out of bed this morning.

He's always dragging violence into the conversation.

6. Paras. 12 – 13.

Q: What does the author mean by the sentence "Surely Miss McVee hadn't crossed into the enemy camp, too"?

A: Miss McVee was the author's favourite teacher, who had obviously been kinder to her than the other teachers. This sentence suggests that the author was beginning to suspect that Miss McVee had joined them because she "ordered her" to come and sit in the front row, directly before her. The author probably thought that Miss McVee was going to punish her for what she was wearing. The word "surely" actually suggests that she was not sure that Miss McVee "hadn't crossed into the enemy camp".

Discussion:
- How many times did I feel an impulse to cry?
- Why did I try hard to hold tears back every time?

◇ Worksheet:

A: As usual the author came to class depressed after assembly. She was thinking of recovering and regaining her composure by losing herself in a novel at the back of the classroom when she was ordered to sit in the front row, which she thought was an omen for another humiliation.

composure *n*. the feeling of being calm, confident, and relaxed

e.g. You may feel nervous but don't lose composure in front of her.

She looked remarkably composed throughout the funeral.

7. Paras. 14 – 17.

Q: Why does the author say that "The block of ice that was my young heart thawed instantly"?

A: The author implies that her heart had been frozen by the umpteen cold humiliations in the school and that she was immensely moved by Miss McVee's warm words. To the author's surprise, Miss McVee did not do anything to humiliate her. Instead she uttered "the most welcome sentence" the author had ever heard in the school.

Discussion:
- How were Miss McVee's words delicate and encouraging?
- What does a teacher's praise mean in the class?
- Does Miss McVee act in character?
- Actually, not every girl is as lucky as the author. Can you imagine an alternative ending?

thaw *vi.* to (cause to) change from a solid, frozen state to a liquid or soft one, because of an increase in temperature; to become friendlier or more relaxed

e.g. The report shows that relations between the two countries thawed a little after the talks.

III. Appreciating the Language

1. Writing feature.

(1) Spot the words that indicate the author's feelings and track down her emotional change.

(2) What devices are employed by the author to convey her feelings?

(3) Can you identify some pattern? What effect is achieved?

A: In the passage a number of expressions and sentences are employed to indicate the ups and downs of the author's emotions and feelings. The following expressions and sentences are used to indicate the author's emotions:

课堂教学安排	*Every day I would battle back tears …* *… I had no choice but to see the punishment through.* Watch the micro-lecture in Chapter 1.2.6. 2. Rhetoric devices. (1) Watch the micro-lecture in Chapter 7.3.1. (2) Identify the rhetoric devices employed in the following sentences. • *Times were tough, money was short, anxiety was rife and the pawnshop was a familiar destination.* • *My sturdy and ingenious father could turn his hand to almost anything.* • *While Mum had scrimped and saved to obtain most of the gear, I still didn't have the prescribed blue blazer and hatband.* • *Every day I would be pulled out of line and made to stand on the stage as a shining example of what not to wear to school.* (3) Find more examples of the above devices from supplementary materials in online course. 3. Applying the strategy. (1) Rewrite the text from Miss McVee's perspective. Try to apply the rhetoric devices to convey the protagonist's feelings. (2) Adapt it to a playwright and act it out in class. 4. Exploring the theme. (1) What would you do in the following scenarios? • A student goes to the wrong classroom and sits there. • A student's stomach growls in the quiet classroom. • A student performs rather poorly in the exam. • A student behaves inappropriately. (2) Watch movies *Dead Poets' Society* and *Mona Lisa Smile* and summarize the teaching wisdom in each movie. (3) Write a journal of reflection on what you learn from the text.

教学反思

本单元的主题是"好老师对学生的影响",通过课堂导入时的头脑风暴、视频讨论和经历分享,同学们对"何为好老师"有了自己的标准和解读。之后在围绕文本内容的启发式提问、小组讨论中,学生将自己代入课文语境中的主人公角色,感受语言背后传递的内心情感,深刻理解了老师在关键时一句鼓励的话足以改变学生的一生,正所谓"良言三冬暖"。

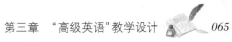

2. Book 6 Unit 2 Bards of the Internet

课程名称	高级英语	教学对象	英语专业三年级学生
学时安排	4学时		
教学目标	Students will be able to: 1. infer tips of quoting others; 2. identify the cohesive devices and various rhetoric devices; 3. figure out the logic pattern of the text; 4. conduct rhetoric analysis of an argument; 5. weigh pros and cons of online writing; 6. spot and stop fake news.		
教学思想	1. Close reading based on textual evidence. 2. Collaborative and autonomous learning. 3. Integration of language skills, humanity and critical thinking.		
教学分析			
教学内容	Lead-in, structural analysis, cohesive devices, writing strategies		
教学重点	Structural analysis, logic pattern and various quotes		
教学难点	A number of cultural notes, cohesive devices		
教学方法	Group discussion, lead-in video, Socratic questions, sharing experience, worksheet, online test		
教学过程			
课堂教学安排	I. Approaching the Topic 1. Lead-in activities. (1) Brainstorming. • What do you think of the exhibit? • What is your understanding of the cover? • What are the biggest fears of our generation? (2) Watch the TED videos and fill in the following blanks. ◇ Modern people are unable to control how much time they spent online, and this psychological _____ may result in degradation in white matter which controls emotional _____, attention and _____. Social media provides _____ with little effort required, and our brain desires for more _____.		

◇ Ironically, those who constantly switch between work and websites perform much worse _____ during tests. The increased online communication reduces ability to _____ out _____. Our brains perceive each _____ as from our phones and our brain has been _____ in a way that has never before in history. It turns out that 80% of social media communication is _____. And the brain parts related to motivation and love are stimulated even more when we know there is an _____. Studies of relationship find that partners tend to like each other more and there are _____ increases of partnership that started online.

(3) Answer the following questions.
- What is wrong with our conversation?
- How does technology influence our mind?
- What are the three fantasies?
- What can be done to address those fantasies?

Discussion:

◇ Mc Luhan once said, "We shape our tools and thereafter our tools shape us." To what extent do you agree or disagree?

◇ We have become accustomed to communicating with each other through social media like WeChat. The Internet has changed our life one way or another. Please share an example on how the Internet has changed your life.

2. Author's background.

Q1: What do you know about Phillip Elmer-Dewitt?

Q2: How does his background influence his opinion?

Q3: How does he describe his bonding with Apple products?

A: Phillip Elmer-DeWitt is a senior editor of *Time* magazine. Since 1982, Elmer-DeWitt has written about science and technology for the magazine. As a staff writer for that publication, he has launched two new sections in the magazine: in 1982, "Computers" and in 1987, "Technology". In 1993, Elmer-DeWitt also spearheaded *Time* Online, the interactive edition of the magazine. Elmer-DeWitt has produced over four hundred news and feature stories on a wide range of subjects. He is currently writing a daily blog called Apple 3.0.

3. Title interpretation.

Online discussion:

- Which words pop up in your mind when it comes to the Internet?
- What is the meaning of "bards"? How is "Internet" related to "bards"?
- How do you interpret the title?
- How does the title function structurally?

A: A storyteller or verse-maker employed by a patron to commemorates the patron's ancestors and the patron's own activities.

II. Analyzing the Text

1. Writing purpose.

Decide which of the following best states the author's purpose.

A. To offer a general view on the merits and demerits of online writing and related matters.

B. To express his disapproval of the foolish and trivial writings on the Internet.

C. To give a historical review on net writing and its impact on younger generations.

2. Structural analysis.

(1) Order the list of headings.

    A. Another merit of net writing

    B. Net writing VS professional writing

    C. In defense of net writing

    D. Criteria for good net writing

    E. Deviation not rare in history

    F. Analytical comparison

    G. Poor quality and underlying reasons

(2) Draw the structural map and identify the logic pattern.

A: The author describes the current fashion for net writing (Paras. 1–3), explores the causes of the poor quality of writing found on the Internet (Paras. 4–6), and explains its merits and differences from published writing (Paras. 7–11) as well as justifications for its survival and prevalence (Paras. 12–13).

(3) Complete the worksheet of text overview.

  ◇ Genre and writing purpose

  ◇ Biographical data of the author

  ◇ Structural analysis

  ◇ Writing features

(4) Teacher's illustration and feedback.

  ◇ Clarify students' confusion

  ◇ Restate the key points

3. Close reading.

(1) Paras. 1–3.

Q1: Why does the author relate what happened to the telephone with what is happening to the computer?

A: By doing so, the author seems to suggest that writing, which went out of style with the invention of the telephone, is experiencing an unexpected comeback with online letter writing.

Q2: What is implied when the author says "the media of Mc Luhan were supposed to render obsolete the medium of Shakespeare"?

A: The phrase "the media of Mc Luhan" refers to the new media that became popular in the 20th century such as radio, television and movies, while "the medium of Shakespeare" refers to the traditional way of "letter writing" in the main clause of this sentence. The sentence implies that, instead of being rendered obsolete, letter writing is experiencing the fastest development since the 18th century, though it is in the "online" form.

Q3: What does the author mean when he says "E-mail and computer conferencing is teaching an entire generation about the flexibility and utility of prose"?

A: The author means that E-mail and computer conferencing demonstrates to a whole generation of people that the language we use does not have to be always so formal as in traditional letter writing; it can be used in a casual manner while still serving its purpose effectively.

Q4: What does the author wish to convey in his comparison between net writing with "scribblers' compacts", Mark Twain's discovery of new journalism in San Francisco, Revolutionary War pamphleteers and the achievements of the Elizabethan era? And what does he find with his comparison?

A: The author uses these examples to tell the readers that there are some similarities between net writing and those experimental, even innovative writing modes in history, and so net writing could be regarded as a kind of renaissance.

Discussion:

- Given a choice between a text and voice message, what would you do? Why?
- What is Mc Luhan's claim? Why are "media of Luhan" in plural form but "medium of Shakespeare" in singular form?
- How are the quotations sequenced in this paragraph?
- What writing strategies does the author employ in this paragraph?

◇ Worksheet:

Spot the people and quotation in Para. 3, match them with the points in the right column and induce the tips for quoting.

A: The first two paragraphs are an introductory lead-in that presents an analytical comparison between what happened to writing when the telephone was invented and what is happening on computer networks now. In Para. 3, a number of people's remarks are quoted. These quotations serve as evidence of the fact that deviations from the traditional medium of letter writing are not rare in history. The implication is that we should not be surprised by the boom in net writing.

render *vt.* to cause someone or something to be in a particular condition; to express, show, or perform something in a particular way

e.g. His rudeness rendered me speechless.

　　The singers rendered the song with enthusiasm.

(2) Paras. 4–6.

Q: What are the reasons that could account for the poor quality of net writing?

A: First, things (such as E-mails) written on the Internet have little literary value, so they're not meant to be permanent. They just come and go and no one will ever remember them, once they are read. Second, many online postings are produced under great time pressure. Third, there is actually no threshold on the Internet, so that anyone can log on and send out what they have written.

Discussion:

- How does the 1st sentence function in Para. 4?
- What do you think of the example?
- Translate the 3rd and 4th sentences in Para. 5.
- Can you identify the contrast in Para. 6?

◇ Worksheet:

Spot the textual evidence and identify the strategy used to illustrate the three reasons.

sloppy *a.* lacking care or effort

e.g. Spelling mistakes always look sloppy in a formal letter.

　　Another sloppy pass like that might lose them the whole match.

(3) Paras. 7–11.

Q1: What is implied in the sentence "… when I met Mark I was dressed as the Canterbury Tales. Rather difficult to do as you might suspect, but I wanted to make a certain impression"?

A: "I was dressed as the Canterbury Tales" means "I was dressed in a very old-fashioned medieval style". The whole sentence suggests that Green wanted to attract attention.

Q2: What are the criteria for good writing favored by the Internet?

A: Good writing on the net should be clear, witty and brief. Units of thought are to be found in short paragraphs, bulleted lists and one-liners.

Q3: What does the author mean by "what works on the computer networks isn't necessarily what works on paper"?

Discussion:

- What are the reasons accounting for good net writing? Do you agree?
- Distinguish "moribund" from "dying". Why does the author use "critiquing" instead of "criticizing"?

- How do net writers differ from professional writers?
- Do you think net writing will ever replace traditional writing? Why or why not?
- Can you relate to your experience and talk about another merit of net writing?

◇ Worksheet:

A: In Para. 7, the author begins to cite examples in defense of net writing. He first points out that there are actually some really good writings on the Internet. In Paras. 8 – 9, the author discusses two reasons why there are some "gems" on the Internet: One is that only good writing will survive; and the other is the "collaborative" work in computer conferences. In Para. 10, the author explains one of the distinguishing features of net writing, which, however, does not detract from its quality. In Para. 11, the author mentions another merit of the Internet, which allows thousands of common people to take up the craft of writing.

prevail *v.* to be common among a group of people or in an area at a particular time

e. g. I am sure that common sense will prevail in the end.

This attitude still prevails among the middle classes.

come across: to make an impression on people who meet them or are listening to them

e. g. She comes across really well on television.

What comes across in his later poetry is a great sense of sadness.

enfranchise *v.* to give someone the right to vote

e. g. Women in Britain were first enfranchised in 1918.

(4) Paras. 12 – 13.

Q1: How does the author justify the legitimacy of net writing?

A: The author contends that net writing may seem foolish and trivial, but most people's lives are foolish and trivial. For millions of people those networks represent a living, breathing life of letters.

Q2: Who does "the Bard" refer to in the last sentence? And how does it differ from the "Bards" in the title?

A: "The Bard" refers to William Shakespeare, while "Bards" in the title refers to the people who write on the Internet. It appears that the author suggests by the title that the medium of net writing, like that of Shakespeare, is perfectly justifiable. The medium changes with the time, so does the "bard".

Discussion:

- How does Para. 12 function? Is it necessary?
- Why does the author mention Brook Farm and the Globe Theatre?

◇ Worksheet:

A: The last two paragraphs present a counter-argument to one of the criticisms against net writing, that is, "It's easy to make this stuff look foolish and trivial". According to Nielsen Hayden, "a lot of everyone's daily life is foolish and trivial," and besides, net writing represents "for millions of people, a living, breathing life of letters".

III. Appreciating the Language

1. Writing feature.

(1) In this passage the author uses a number of quotations in support of his ideas and opinions. Try to find what sources the author quotes, explain what ideas these quotations are used to support and figure out some tips of quoting others.

A: In Para. 3 the author quotes the following persons in support of the idea that E-mail and net writing could be compared to the writings in history that were experimental and flexible in nature: Jon Carroll, a columnist at the San Francisco Chronicle; Patrick Nielsen Hayden, an editor at Tor Books; David Sewell, an associate editor at the University of Arizona. In Paras. 5 and 6, the author quotes the following persons to explore the reasons for the poor quality of writing on the Internet: Gerard Van der Leun, literary agent based in Westport, Connecticut; Mary Anne Mohanraj, a Chicago-based poet. In Para. 8, the author quotes the following persons in his discussion of the criteria to judge the quality of net writing: Jorn Barger, a software designer in Chicago; Crawford Kilian, a writing teacher at Capilano College in Vancouver, British Columbia.

(2) Look up the following cultural notes online, figure out the purposes they serve and present your findings to the class.

	Cultural Notes
Para. 2	media of Mc Luhan, medium of Shakespeare
Para. 3	scribblers' compacts, literary scene in San Francisco in the 1860s, Tom Paine, Revolutionary War, Elizabethan Era, Gutenberg
Para. 7	mock-epic, *Canterbury Tales*
Para. 9	WELL, *New York Time*, *Wall Street Journal*
Para. 12	Des Moines, VIXEN
Para. 13	Brook Farm, Globe Theater, the Bard

(3) Watch the micro-lecture "How to read an argumentative essay" and identify the rhetoric appeals employed in the text with textual evidence.

(4) Watch the micro-lecture "Cohesive devices" in Chapter 7.5.1, spot the linguistic cohesion in the text and draw the mind map to visualize the logic pattern.

2. Rhetoric devices.

(1) Watch the micro-lecture "Parody" in Chapter 7.7.3, identify the figurative speeches employed in the following sentences and finish the online quiz in assignment section.
- They're not to have and hold; they're to fire and forget.
- People then were given a choice between picking up a pen or a phone.

(2) Grammatically analyze the following sentences and translate them into Chinese.

Para. 11: *There is something inherently democratizing—perhaps even revolutionary—about the technology. Not only has it enfranchised thousands of would-be writers who otherwise might never have taken up the craft, but it has also thrown together classes of people who hadn't had much direct contact before: students, scientists, senior citizens, computer geeks, grassroots (and often blue-collar) bulletin-board enthusiasts and most recently the working press.*

Para. 13: *But it would be a mistake to dismiss the computer-message boards or to underestimate the effect a lifetime of dashing off e-mail will have on a generation of young writers.*

IV. Applying the Strategy

(1) Read the supplementary materials in Chapter 2.2.8 and establish your individualized expression bank.

(2) Write a body paragraph on one of the following topics and apply at least one rhetoric appeal in your writing:
- How does technology change the relationship between people?
- Will online writing ever replace traditional writing?
- How do social media shape people's lifestyle?

V. Exploring the Theme

(1) Read the supplementary excerpts in the online course and talk about your understanding of Mc Luhan's quote "The medium is the message".

(2) Translate the following passages into English.

◇ 网络是一个民主的平台，所有人都可以发声，但要学会倾听不同的声音。至少应该保持对他人的尊重，因为一旦理智的讨论被迫失声，淹没在众多谩骂、诽谤、人身攻击中，网络就会变成情绪的垃圾桶。

◇ 此外，应区分事实与观点，过滤掉各种道听途说、主观臆断和宣传软文，不要让偏见蒙蔽自己的判断，这很重要，但并非易事。可如果不这么做，对于无知和狭隘照单全收，则绝不可行。

课堂教学安排	(3) Case study. • Compared with maturity of online literature, what happens to common net writers? Do they share similar development with online literature? • What results in people's fading interest in online writing? • Nowadays, rumors, gossips and fake news go viral and prevail online. How can we spot and stop the fake news?

教学反思

  本单元的主题是"网络写作的利与弊",作者指出这种新的写作形式在某种程度上激起了人们的写作热情,网络文学不乏精品,且具有与生俱来的民主性。但另一方面,因网络写作门槛低,网络写作质量堪忧:文法不通,结构混乱,言之无物,充满漫骂和攻击。最后作者总结道,网络写作毕竟代表了年轻一代的生活方式,其存在具有一定的合理性。文章思辨性较强,具有一定的难度,因此课堂教学中教师应注重搭建不同梯度的动态支架,通过多样的活动和任务,循序渐进地引导学生领悟作者的逻辑和技巧。

3. Book 6 Unit 9 How to Grow Old

课程名称	高级英语	教学对象	英语专业三年级学生
学时安排	4 学时		
教学目标	The students will be able to: 1. explore the virtues of growing old and view aging critically; 2. interpret the title and author's quotes; 3. grammatically analyze the complex sentences; 4. appreciate the simile of the theme; 5. detect the author's tone throughout the text; 6. identify the various writing strategies employed in the text.		
教学思想	1. Close reading based on textual evidence. 2. Collaborative and autonomous learning. 3. Integration of language skills, humanity and critical thinking.		
教学分析			
教学内容	Lead-in; generic features and structure; author's tone; writing strategies		
教学重点	Simile of the theme		
教学难点	Author's tone		
教学方法	Group discussion, interpretation of quote, Socratic questions, class presentation, worksheet, comparative analysis		
教学过程			
课堂教学安排	**I. Approaching the Topic** 1. Lead-in activities. (1) Brainstorming: Which words pop up in your mind when it comes to "old"? (2) Analyze the word cloud based on your responses and induce some key words. (3) Online discussion: • What is the social attitude towards old age? • How is it reflected in aspects of life? • Can you think of some virtues of growing old? (4) Listen to the song "When You Are Old" and fill the blanks. What is the tone conveyed in the song?		

课堂教学安排	*When you are old and tired and ________* *Wear your overcoat on sunny days* *When your ________ have all been told* *I'll ask for them when you are old* *When you are old and full of sleep* *And death no longer makes you ________* *When your body ________ with cold* *I'll warm your heart when you are old* *You'll still be the same to me* *A ________ and a ________* *And I will be able to see* *I'll need someone to comfort me* *When you are old and ________ and ________* *A ________ hand is all you want* *I will give you mine to hold* *And I'll be here when you are old* *Yes I will give you mine to hold* *And I'll be here when you are old* 2. Author's background. Q1: What do you know about Bertrand Arthur Russell? A: Bertrand Arthur Russell (1872—1970) was a British philosopher and mathematician who combined scholarship with literary skills and had a rare talent for popularization both in writing and as a broadcaster. On politics and education he held unorthodox opinions. In 1918 he was galled for pacifism. Undeterred by age, he was active in nuclear disarmament demonstrations, which led to another spell in prison. He left Cambridge in the summer of 1894. In the autumn of 1920 he went to China to lecture on philosophy at Peking University, analyzing the strength and weaknesses of that ancient civilization attempting to industrialize, and warned of the dangers of imperial powers interfering in China affairs. In 1950, Russell was awarded the Nobel Prize in Literature, "in recognition of his varied and significant writings in which he champions humanitarian ideals and freedom of thought". ● Read the following quotes of Bertrand Russell and induce the core values conveyed in them. ◇ Three passions, simple but overwhelmingly strong, have governed my life: the longing for love, the search for knowledge and unbearable pity for the suffering of mankind.

◇ The most valuable things in life are not measured in monetary terms. The really important things are not houses and lands, stocks and bonds, automobiles and real state, but friendships, trust, confidence, empathy, mercy, love and faith.

◇ When you want to teach children to think, you begin by treating them seriously when they are little, giving them responsibilities, talking to them candidly, providing privacy and solitude for them, and making them readers and thinkers of significant thoughts from the beginning. That's if you want to teach them to think.

3. Title interpretation.

Q1: Is the text about the aging process, as the title literally shows?

Q2: What is the text actually about?

Q3: Is there a secret formula on keeping young?

A: In the essay, the author turns this social issue of aging into a personal discussion on two topics: How to keep oneself psychologically young and how to perceive death in one's old age.

II. Analyzing the Text

1. Writing purpose.

Decide which of the following best states the author's purpose.

A. To explore the reasons why people usually fear death in old age.

B. To supply some medical information about health and genetic influence on one's longevity.

C. To offer suggestions on how to keep open-minded and make some psychological adjustments in the process of growing old.

2. Structural analysis.

Divide the text into three parts and summarize the main idea for each.

Part 1

(Paras. 1 – 2) Description of the healthy lifestyle of author's ancestors and himself, which reflects his attitude towards life.

Part 2

(Paras. 3 – 4) Two things elderly people should avoid, namely living in memories and clinging to youth.

Part 3

(Paras. 5 – 6) Importance of developing impersonal interests, and a correct attitude towards death in old age.

III. Close Reading

1. Paras. 1 – 2.

Q1: What does the author mean when he says that "But speaking as one of the seventy-two, I prefer her recipe"?

A: My parents were the most enterprising and optimistic ones one could expect to find. The author thinks that her parents did all they could to support the family with their hard work, ingenuity and thrift, and that the family enjoyed "bucketloads of cheer".

Q2: How, according to the author, can one be relieved from the worry of aging?

A: According to the author, if you have wide and keen interests and you participate in activities which you are still capable of, just as his maternal grandmother did, you will have no time to notice that you are growing old and thus you will have no reason to worry about your old age and the probable brevity of your future.

Discussion:

- How many relatives are mentioned in Para. 1? How old are they respectively?
- Why does the author mention the Italian gentleman?

◇ Worksheet:

A: In Para. 1 the author begins the essay with a humorous answer to the question "How not to grow old?"—"To choose your ancestors carefully." Then he tells us some anecdotes about one of his ancestors—his maternal grandmother, who enjoyed a long life partly because she had a healthy attitude towards life. In Para. 2 the author gives us a very brief description of his healthy lifestyle, which reflects his attitude towards life.

relate *vt.* to tell a story or describe an event

e. g. She related the events of the past week to the police.

He relates how at the age of 23 he was interned in the prison camp.

2. Paras. 3 – 4.

Q1: How could one get out of undue absorption in the past?

A: To get oneself out of undue absorption in the past, one must direct one's thought to the future and to the things about which there is something to be done.

Q2: How, according to the author, should an elderly person show his concern for his children?

A: An elderly person should avoid showing too much interest in his children when they are grown up and want to live their own lives. He should be thoughtful and be ready to give them help only when they need it.

Discussion:

Why does the author mention animals and their young in Para. 4?

◇ Worksheet:

A: After talking about his ancestors' longevity and his own healthy lifestyle, the author directs his discussion to the two things elderly people should avoid, namely living in memories and clinging to youth, which are interrelated, because undue absorption in the past would inevitably lead to clinging to youth.

undue *a.* not necessary or reasonable

e.g. Such a high increase will impose an undue burden on the local tax payer.

It's difficult to find a way of spreading information about the disease without causing undue alarm.

3. Paras. 5 – 6.

Q1: What, according to the author, should "those who are incapable of impersonal interests" realize?

A: Those who are incapable of impersonal interests should realize that their undue interest in their children is unwelcome, though their "material services" are still appreciated.

Q2: What is the best way for an old person to overcome the fear of death?

A: First of all, he should realize that death is inevitable. The best way to overcome the fear of death is to develop strong impersonal interests involving appropriate activities, so that he will painlessly lose his individual being (i.e. his ego) and his life will become merged in the universal life.

Discussion:

● Do you find "growing old" a terrifying process? Why or why not?

◇ Worksheet:

A: In Para. 5 the author stresses the importance of developing impersonal interests. With such interests one will have a fulfilling old age without making his grown-up children feel oppressed. Otherwise, he will either feel empty or unduly concern himself with his children. The last paragraph expounds on a correct attitude towards death in old age. According to the author, death should not be an oppressive problem for "an old man who has known human joys and sorrows". He compares one's life to a river that will eventually be merged with the sea. This metaphor suggests that death is inevitable and, more important, it is part of "the universal life".

oppressive *a.* something that is oppressive makes you feel very worried or anxious

e.g. an oppressive silence; oppressive weather

Several people had experienced the same oppressive feeling when they slept in that room.

IV. Appreciating the Language

1. Writing feature.

(1) In the last paragraph the author compares one's life to a river with its different phases. Watch the micro-lecture "Mind Map" in Chapter 1.2.6, draw a bridge map to illustrate the similarities and describe how this simile works for the theme of the essay.

A: The metaphor is used to illustrate particular characteristics of an individual human existence in three different phases:

- When people are young, they are more vigorous and energetic ("rushing passionately past rocks and over waterfalls"), but less experienced ("small" "contained within its banks").
- When they reach their middle age, they have got more experience and wisdom ("Gradually the river grows wider, the banks recede …") and their pace of life becomes more gentle but steady ("… the waters flow more quietly …").
- As their sense of fulfillment increases in old age, their sense of individuality decreases, and their lives become increasingly blended with the universal life ("become merged in the sea" "lose their individual being").

(2) Think-pair-share: Life is like a/an _____.

(3) Detect the author's tone and justify with textual evidence.

Para. 1: "*My first advice would be to choose your ancestors carefully.*"

"*But speaking as one of the seventy-two …*"

"*… you will have no reason to think about the merely statistical fact …*"

Para. 2: "*… though in actual fact the things I like doing are mostly wholesome.*"

Para. 3: "*Psychologically there are two dangers to be guarded against in old age.*"

(4) What writing strategies are employed to elaborate on the author's suggestion?

(5) The author uses "I" "my" in Para. 1, but he uses "one" "one's" in Para. 3 and "you" or "your" in Paras. 4 to 6. Notably, the shift of addressing forms has some specific functions. Spot the places where the author addresses the readers in different forms and explain the functions of such shifts.

A: The shift shortens the distance between the readers and the issue under discussion. When he uses "you" and "your", the author draws the readers closer to the relevant issues, since what is discussed concerns all of you. Also, it creates an intimacy of having a direct conversation. Thus, the issues are rendered with a wider significance that is not merely limited to "I".

2. Rhetoric devices.

(1) Watch the micro-lecture "Parallel Structure" in Chapter 7.3.1 and identify the paralleled sentences in the text.

(2) Identify the rhetoric devices used in the following sentences.

• My maternal grandfather, it is true, was cut off in the flower of his youth at the age of sixty-seven.

(3) Grammatically analyze the following sentences and translate them into Chinese.

• I do not mean that one should be without interest in them, but one's interest should be contemplative and, if possible, philanthropic, but not unduly emotional.

• Young men who have reason to fear that they will be killed in battle may justifiably feel bitter in the thought that they have been cheated of the best things that life has to offer.

(4) Pay attention to the underlined words and see how their meaning is different in the context.

• She used to <u>relate</u> how she met in Italy an elderly gentleman who was looking very sad.

• This, I think, is the proper <u>recipe</u> for remaining young.

V. Applying the Strategy

Apply the parallel structure and translate the following into English.

我公司拟招聘具备以下条件的员工：
——本科学历
——至少五年工作经验
——英语流利
——会用电脑

VI. Exploring the Theme

(1) Read and appreciate the poem "When You Are Old" by Willian Butler Yeats.

(2) Read the supplementary material "Two Truths to Live By" and analyze how the author's attitude towards life is similar to or different from Bertrand Russell.

(3) Compare the text "How to Grow Old" with "Youth" in Chapter 3.2.7 in terms of theme, writing strategy and author's tone.

(4) Watch the video *How to Grow Old Gracefully* and answer the following questions:

• How can people grow old gracefully?

• How does the video echo the text?

(5) Read the supplementary materials and deliver a speech titled "The Chinese Youth" based on what you have learnt.

教学反思

　　本单元的主题是"如何变老",通过课堂导入时的头脑风暴、在线讨论和音频练习,同学们能够辩证地思考变老的过程,并列出其诸多益处。之后通过围绕文本内容的启发式提问、小组讨论和课堂任务,学生逐步理解作者提出的建议,专注提升自我,练就过硬本领,在追梦路上释放青春激情,勇担时代重任。

4. Book 5 Unit 1 The Fourth of July

课程名称	高级英语	教学对象	英语专业三年级学生
学时安排	4学时		
教学目标	The students will be able to: 1. grasp generic features of autobiography; 2. draw the story map; 3. identify rhetoric devices and writing strategies; 4. infer the logic of ordering events; 5. detect the changes of the author's feelings.		
教学思想	1. Close reading based on textual evidence. 2. Collaborative and autonomous learning. 3. Integration of language skills, humanity and critical thinking.		
教学分析			
教学内容	Generic features, structural analysis, critical reading, writing strategies		
教学重点	Generic features of autobiography, writing strategies		
教学难点	Author's tone, rhetoric devices		
教学方法	Online discussion, lead-in video, Socratic questions, story map, class presentation, worksheet		
教学过程			
课堂教学安排	**I. Approaching the Topic** 1. Lead-in activities. (1) Brainstorming: What are the first words occurring to you when it comes to "discrimination"? (2) Analyze the word cloud based on students' responses and provide relevant theory to facilitate understanding. (3) Watch the video clip, fill in the gaps and answer the following questions. • What is Perry confused about? • What are the dilemmas for the peacock and the penguin respectively? (4) Share your thought on the following excerpts: "The only way to make apartheid work was to cripple the black mind. Under apartheid, the government built what became known as Bantu schools which taught no science, no history, no civics. They taught metrics and agriculture: how to count potatoes, how to pave roads, chop wood, till the soil."		

"It does not serve the Bandu to learn history and science because he is primitive."

"Why educate a slave? Why teach someone Latin when his only purpose is to dig holes in the ground?"

2. Author's background.

Audre Lorde (1934—1992), born in New York, is a Caribbean American, whose emphasis is on oppression, revolution and change. The text is from her autobiography *Zami: A New Spelling of My Name*.

Some of her quotes go as follow: "It is not our differences that divide us. It is our inability to recognize, accept and celebrate those differences." "Your silence will not protect you."

3. Title interpretation.

Q1: What does the title *The Fourth of July* indicate? What is special about that day?

Q2: How does the title function structurally and rhetorically?

Q3: What are the criteria of a good title?

II. Analyzing the Text

1. Writing purpose.

(1) Illustrate the author's purpose.

The writer intends to lay bare or bring to light the white domination or racial discrimination and segregation by vivid specific examples, consequently to convey her fury and indignation.

2. Structural analysis.

(1) Watch the micro-lecture "Autobiography" in Chapter 1.3.7.1 and complete Worksheet 1—the text overview.

(2) Complete the story map.

(3) Present your version to the class and peer review.

- Whether important events are included.
- Whether major conflicts are identified.
- Whether the theme is summarized.

(4) Teacher's illustration and feedback.

- Clarify students' confusion.
- Restate the key points.
- Play the reference version.

Part 1

(Para. 1) The setting (who, when, where, what, why).

Part 2

(Paras. 2 – 7) Preparations before their arrival.

Part 3

(Paras. 8 – 17) Experience of injustice during their stay in Washington D. C.

Part 4

(Paras. 18 – 19) Different reactions afterwards.

3. Close reading.

(1) Paras. 1 – 7.

Q1: What do we know about the family's economic situation?

A: The fact that the family had always traveled on the cheap milk train implies that the family was rather poor.

Q2: How did they feel during the preparation for the trip?

Q3: What does "a mobile feast" mean in Para. 3?

Q4: List the variety of foods "my mom" prepared for the trip.

two roasted chickens	slices of brown bread and butter	green pepper and carrot sticks
iced cakes with scalloped edges	a spice bun and rock cakes	iced tea in a wrapped mayonnaise jar
sweet pickles	dill pickles	peaches with the fuzz still on them

Discussion:

- Why did my mom prepare so much food?
- Is it necessary to list the foods in such a detailed way? What is the author's purpose?
- What can you infer about "my mom"?
- Do Paras. 5 – 7 follow the chronological sequence?
- What is the ordering logic of major events in the text?
- Grammatically analyze the 2nd sentence in Para. 7 and its function.

◇ Worksheet:

A: On the one hand, by taking a variety of food with them on the trip, the family members could save some money, for dining car food was too expensive. On the other hand, as black people, they were not allowed into railroad dining cars at that time. From an alternative perspective, her Christian parents are reputed to have set strict standards and may well have frowned on sunglasses as suggestive of a sinful vanity.

(2) Paras. 8 – 12.

Q1: Why was the author squinting?

A: Because she was suffering realistically from the dazzling sunlight and mentally from the suffocating white domination.

Q2: What images appear frequently in Paras. 8 – 11?

Q3: What is the significance of these images?

Q4: Translate the last two sentences in Para. 12.

Discussion:

- Why did my parents disapprove of sunglasses?
- What was the social background of the US in 1947?
- How were the black people treated back then in the US?
- What is the author's tone in Paras. 8 – 11? Justify with textual evidence.

◇ Worksheet:

A: Besides the expense, her parents wanted their children to realize to the fullest extent the injustice that was inflicted upon the black people, though wearing sunglasses will make the dazzling light milder.

(3) Paras. 13 – 19.

Q1: Why didn't anyone understand the waitress at first?

Q2: Did she really speak in a "loud and clear" voice?

Q3: How did my parents react to the discrimination? How about my sisters?

Q4: Grammatically analyze and translate the 1st sentence in Para. 18.

Discussion:

- Did what happened in Para. 16 surprise you? Why or why not?
- How did the author feel then? Trace her emotional changes throughout the text.

III. Appreciating the Language

1. Writing feature.

(1) Watch the micro-lecture of "Foreshadowing" in Chapter 1.3.7.3 and do the matching exercise.

(2) Identify the writing features of the excerpt from autobiography and justify with textual evidence.

(3) Watch the micro-lecture in Chapter 1.3.7.4, spot more examples of symbolism in the text and analyze their symbolic meaning.

2. Rhetoric devices.

(1) Watch the micro-lecture in Chapter 1.3.8.

(2) Identify the rhetoric devices employed in the following sentences.

- *We went to the fabled and famous capital.*
- *The black family was discriminated on July 4th in Washington D. C.*

(3) Find more examples of the above devices from supplementary materials in the online course.

课堂教学安排	**IV. Applying the Strategy** （1）Rewrite the text from the white waitress' perspective. Try to apply the writing strategies we've learnt to create the conflict. （2）If you were the author, how would you draft the angry letter to the president? **V. Exploring the Theme** ◇ Case study: Find a current issue of cultural stereotypes, provide background information, analyze causes and present your attitude.

教学反思
在实际的教学过程中，小组讨论最初没能有效启动，部分同学不愿提出疑问，讨论或时有跑题，或缺乏对问题原因的深入探讨。教师需要根据学生的语言水平、认知规律和情感需求，巧妙地设计思考和讨论问题，并加强对学生参与讨论和陈述过程的管理，给出明确的评价标准，以利于同伴互评及教师对学生的形成性评价。

5. Book 5 Unit 3 A Hanging

课程名称	高级英语	教学对象	英语专业三年级学生
学时安排	2 学时		
教学目标	The students will be able to: 1. discuss pros and cons of death penalty; 2. infer characteristics of the protagonist; 3. appreciate devices of description.		
教学思想	1. Close reading based on textual evidence. 2. Collaborative and autonomous learning. 3. Integration of language skills, humanity and critical thinking.		
教学分析			
教学内容	Structural analysis, characterization, writing strategies, author's motive		
教学重点	Characterization, description		
教学难点	Writing motive, author's tone		
教学方法	Online discussion, lead-in video, Socratic questions, character sketch, class presentation, worksheet, comparative analysis		
教学过程			
课堂教学安排	**I. Approaching the Topic** 1. Lead-in Activities. (1) Brainstorming • What are the pros and cons of death penalty? • What is the controversy? • Are you a proponent or opponent? (2) Watch the lead-in videos and fill in the following blanks. ◇ Prosecutor: —_____ injected without patients' _____. —_____ _____ cause another human being's death. —That is _____. ◇ Attorney: The case of African elephants: _____, _____, giant creatures become very _____.		

—_____, _____ trauma & stress by poachers and land developers, causing _____ & _____ change to them.

—It was utter _____.

—During that horrendous week, the US was _____ to be _____.

—When the _____ effects started to become clear, and _____ and _____, she stayed with the five patients, each facing a(n) _____, _____ and _____ death, surrounded by pain, _____ and _____ which are _____ to us.

—She never lost her _____ sense of _____.

(3) Discuss the following questions:
- What is the prosecutor's accusation?
- Why does the attorney introduce African elephants?
- How does he defend his client?

2. Author's background.

Q1: What do you know about George Orwell?

Q2: What are his major works?

Q3: How do his life experiences shape his writing?

(1) Match his writing motives with corresponding elaboration.

(2) Create the author's profile and share some of his quotes with the class.

"Minds are like parachutes—they only function when open."

"Man is the only real enemy we have. Remove Man from the scene, and the root cause of hunger and overwork is abolished for ever. Man is the only creature that consumes without producing. He does not give milk, he does not lay eggs, he is too weak to pull the plough, he cannot run fast enough to catch rabbits. Yet he is lord of all the animals. He sets them to work, he gives back to them the bare minimum that will prevent them from starving, and the rest he keeps for himself."

II. Analyzing the Text

1. Structural analysis.

(1) Divide the text into three parts according to the chronological sequence.

Part 1 (Para. 1) Setting (when, where, what, who).

Part 2 (Paras. 2-13) Before the hanging.

Part 3 (Paras. 14-22) After the hanging.

2. Close reading.

(1) Approaching the setting.

Q1: What was the weather like?

Q2: How does the author describe the condemned cells?

Q3: Who are the major characters in the text?

<table>
<tr><td rowspan="2">课
堂
教
学
安
排</td><td>

（2）Approaching the characters.

Q4：How does the author describe each character? Who do you think is the protagonist and who is the antagonist?

Q5：Which paragraph reflects the author's attitude towards hanging?

Q6：Is his thought consistent with his behavior? Why or why not?

Q7：Can you identify some differences before and after the hanging? Justify with textual clues.

Q8：What is the general tone of the text?

Discussion：
- How does the setting contribute to the theme?
- What does "due to be hanged" indicate?
- What can be inferred about the characters based on the textual evidence?
- How is the irony reflected in each character?
- How does the author make the description dynamic?

III. Exploring the Theme

The following questions will be asked to facilitate students' thinking.
- What are George Orwell's four writing motives?
- What is his political purpose in writing the text?
- Which paragraph do you think mostly expresses his stand?

IV. Appreciating the Language
- What point of view is used by the author?
- What tense is mainly employed?
- Are there other devices adopted to make the writing dynamic?

V. Assignments

◇ Watch the micro-lecture on characterization and make inferences about other characters.

</td></tr>
</table>

教学反思

　　由于本单元主题和学生日常生活经验关联甚少，语篇分析时有些学生感觉无话可说，较难依靠自己的经验解读课文，因此，教师设计教学时要注重补充相关的背景资料和多模态的语料，设计有梯度的任务和练习，为学生解读文本搭建"脚手架"，使学生在完成任务或参与教学活动的过程中去感悟与领会，通过理解、分析与思考实现知识内化。此外，设计提问练习时，要有促进分析、应用、整合的高阶提问，激发学生对文本信息的批判性审视，帮助学生从文本使用者成长为文本分析者、文本评论者。

6. Book 5 Unit 5 Superstition

课程名称	高级英语	教学对象	英语专业三年级学生
学时安排	2 学时		
教学目标	The students will be able to: 1. realize the harmful consequences of superstition; 2. master the topic-related expressions; 3. apply rhetorical appeals in arguments.		
教学思想	1. Close reading based on textual evidence. 2. Collaborative and autonomous learning. 3. Integration of language skills, humanity and critical thinking.		
教学分析			
教学内容	Structural analysis, rhetoric appeals, writing strategies		
教学重点	Writing strategies in argument		
教学难点	Three rhetoric appeals		
教学方法	Online discussion, brainstorming, Socratic questions, blank-filling, peer review, worksheet		
教学过程			

课堂教学安排	**I. Approaching the Topic**
	 1. Lead-in activities.
	 ◇ Brainstorming
	  • What are the symptoms of superstition?
	  • Are they auspicious or ominous?
	  • What are the underlying causes?
	 2. Author's background.
	 Q1: What do you know about the author?
	 Q2: How do his life experiences shape his writing?
	 Search for his quotes and share one with the class.
	
	 Inspect every piece of pseudoscience and you will find a security blanket.
	 — Isaac Asimov —		

3. Interpret the title.

◇ Discussion:

Q1: What is the fight against?

Q2: Why is it never-ending?

II. Analyzing the Text

1. Structural analysis.

◇ Divide the text into parts and fill in the blanks.

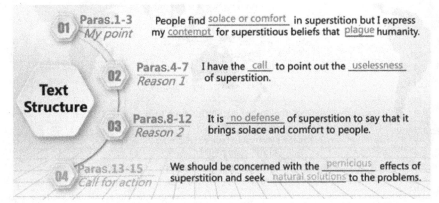

2. Close reading.

(1) Watch the micro-lecture "Rhetoric Appeals" in Chapter 7.2.

(2) Complete the following worksheet.

Paras.	Signal words	Strategy employed	Rhetorical appeal
4	... the call to preach my version of ...		
5,6	Unlike ... Rather ...		
8	It is no defense of superstition to say that ...		
9	If ..., there is no behavior we ought to interfere with.		
10	Can it not be argued that ...?		
11	There is indeed something to this ... But ...		
14,15	We live in ... ... all threaten us ...		

(3) Present your version to the class and justify with textual evidence.

<table>
<tr><td rowspan="2">课堂教学安排</td><td>

III. Exploring the Theme

The following questions will be asked to facilitate students' thinking.

- What is the author's attitude towards superstition?
- What are the harmful effects of superstition?
- How is the author's belief echoed in the text?

IV. Assessing the Logic

◇ Discuss the validity of the author's argument, using the following table as the reference.

Checklist for writing	Scale 1 2 3 4 5	Comment
1. Does the author cite any facts or statistics?		
2. Is the argument logic?		
3. Does the author invoke any emotion from the readers?		
4. Does the author convey his tone to the readers?		
5. Does the author establish credibility in the argument?		
6. Does the author show himself as unbiased and trustworthy?		

V. Assignments

◇ Relate to your personal experiences, point out the harmful effects of superstition and advocate rational solutions to the problems.

</td></tr>
</table>

教学反思

教师需要深入挖掘文章的主题及其文化内涵,并联系实际展开案例分析,从而体现教学内容的时代性和前沿性。教师要善于捕捉语篇内容与社会问题或与学生经历密切相关的契合点,并设计情境问题,组织学生讨论,鼓励他们对一些社会现象进行比较、阐释、质疑及论证,使学生感到所学是和社会现象及个人生活息息相关、有诸多共性的,从而激发他们的深层学习动机。

第四章

"口译理论与实践"教学设计

1. Educational Interpreting: Astronomy Photographer of the Year

课程名称	口译理论与实践	教学对象	英语专业三年级学生
学时安排	1学时		
教学目标	**Knowledge Objectives** 1. Know the tips for the preparation before translation. 2. Understand the features of note-taking. **Ability Objectives** 1. Analyze the features of qualified interpretation notes. 2. Be able to write notes by using some arrows, symbols and abbreviations. **Emotion Objectives** 1. Draw inspiration and strength from the winner of the 2021 Astronomy Photographer. 2. A growing interest in learning the note-taking skills.		
教学思想	The teaching of interpretation is based on the ideas of flipped classroom. Before the class, the teacher gives the students the video of *Astronomy Photographer of the Year* and asks them to upload their note-taking and their interpretation on the online course platform. During the class, the teacher summarizes their common problems and discusses with them the interpretation skills such as the note-taking skills. After class, the teacher gives feedbacks to students' homework through the online learning platform.		
教学分析			
教学内容	Preparation before interpretation Flipped classroom: *Astronomy Photographer of the Year* Interpreting skills: note-taking skills		
教学重点	Understand the features of note-taking		
教学难点	Be able to write notes by using arrows, symbols and abbreviations		
教学方法	Flipped classroom; blended learning		
教学过程			
课堂教学安排	**Step 1　Preparation Before Interpretation** Ⅰ. **Knowledge Preparation** Thematic knowledge and language knowledge points.		

Ⅱ. Listening and Translation

Distinguish the primary and secondary relations and internal relations of ideas.

Astronomy Photographer of the Year

Shuchang Dong captured the solar eclipse on June 21st, 2020, in his photography work "The Golden Ring", becoming the winner of the 2021 Astronomy Photographer of the Year competition.

Key words:

tussle:争斗

e.g. There was such a tussle to the finish line.

be united with 与……一致

e.g. We were all united with this particular image.

Step 2　Flipped Classroom

＊ **Students' Scores**

Highest score:91

Average score:80

Lowest score:70

＊ **Common Problems**

(1) I don't think I've ever heard the judges quite as argumentative as they were for this category.

"argumentative"翻译成"辩论,吵架"吗?

(2) Pick the best image and at the end of the day …

"at the end of the day"翻译成"一天结束的时候"吗?

Ⅰ. Sentence Interpretation

The winner of the 2021 Astronomy Photographer of the Year competition is "The Golden Ring" by Shuchang Dong from China, the winner of the category, our Sun.

This was astonishing in the judging session. I don't think I've ever heard the judges quite as argumentative as they were for this category.

There was such a tussle to the finish line.

At the end of the day, we are trying to pick the best image and at the end of the day, we were all united with this particular image.

Ⅱ. Key Points Analysis

(1) I don't think I've ever heard the judges quite as argumentative as they were for this category.

argumentative 可以翻译成"讨论得热火朝天"而不是"辩论"。

(2) Pick the best image and at the end of the day …

at the end of the day 不是"一天结束的时候",而是"最终"的意思。可参考"You are the last person I want to see."("你是我最不想见的人。"而不是"你是我最后一个想见的人。")

Ⅲ. Class Activity

How many times did you listen to the material?

Please type your answers on the online teaching platform.

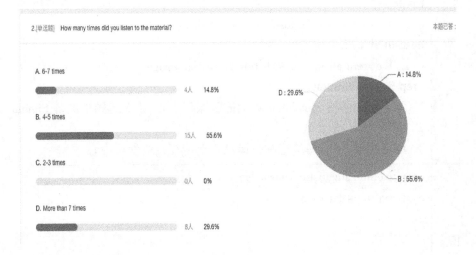

Step 3 Note-taking Skills

Please look at the teacher's demo on the blackboard and summarize the tips for note-taking.

* **Features of Note-taking**
- Vertical arrangement
- Separation of the sense group
- Proper use of arrows, symbols and abbreviation

课堂教学安排	*** Note-taking Practice** Solar eclipses have been capturing the interest of humans for thousands of years across the world. This image demonstrates both the beauty and simplicity of an eclipse, but also the science behind this astronomical event. 千百年来，日食总会吸引全人类的目光。这幅作品不仅彰显了日食的美，尽显其简单的本质，也展现出这一天文现象背后的科学道理。  **Step 4　Summary** ● Vertical arrangement ● Separation of the sense group ● Proper use of arrows, symbols and abbreviation **tussle**：争斗 e. g. There was such a tussle to the finish line. **be united with** 一致 e. g. We were all united with this particular image. **Step 5　Assignments** 1. 第 4 组同学将 Simulation 4 上传至课程中心，第 5 组同学准备 Simulation 5。 2. 视译 P. 58 的课文。 3. 听译视频，将听译笔记和口译录音上传至在线学习中心。
板书设计	cognitive and linguistic knowledge captured the solar eclipse astronomy **Features of Note-taking** Vertical arrangement Separation of the sense group Proper use of arrows, symbols and abbreviation
教学反思	

Students' reflection on the course

1. Students find the reflection on one's note-taking is useful and helps them to see their future room for improvement.

2. Students find doing note-taking on their own during this stage is still a bit challenging and they need more practice after class.

Teacher's reflection on the course

Students' note-taking shows that many students still have some difficulties in writing down the symbols. Most of them have the tendency to write down the whole words, which prevents them from listening to the next sentence.

2. Business Interpreting: Olympic Economy

课程名称	口译理论与实践	教学对象	英语专业三年级学生
学时安排	1学时		
教学目标	**Knowledge Objectives** 1. Know some English expressions relating to Beijing Olympic Mascot. **Ability Objectives** 1. Summarize the features of qualified interpretation notes. 2. Be able to write down interpretation notes by using arrows. **Emotion Objectives** 1. Have an interest in Beijing Olympic Mascot and have faith in the development of winter sports in China. 2. A growing interest in learning interpretation.		
教学思想	The teaching of interpretation is based on the ideas of flipped classroom. Before the class, the teacher gives the students the video of *Bing Dwen Dwen* and asks them to upload their note-taking and their interpretation on the online course platform. During the class, the teacher summarizes their common problems and discusses with them the interpretation skills such as the note-taking skills. After class, the teacher gives comments on students' assignments through online learning platform.		
教学分析			
教学内容	Preparation before interpretation Flipped classroom: Bing Dwen Dwen Interpreting skills: note-taking skills		
教学重点	Know some English expressions relating to Beijing Olympic Mascot		
教学难点	Be able to write down interpretation notes by using arrows		
教学方法	Flipped classroom; blended learning		
教学过程			
课堂教学安排	**Step 1　Preparation Before Interpretation** Ⅰ. **Knowledge Preparation** Thematic knowledge and language knowledge points. Ⅱ. **Listening and Translation** Distinguish the primary and secondary relations and internal relations of ideas.		

课堂教学安排

∗ **Background Knowledge**

Bing Dwen Dwen, the cute mascot of the Beijing 2022 Winter Olympics, has been selling like hotcakes. Why is the ice-glazed panda so popular? What are the ingenious ideas behind its design?

The topic tagged Bing Dwen Dwen had attracted 4.8 billion views on Sina Weibo. Daily sales of the mascot hit a record high of nearly 3 million *yuan*.

∗ **Translate the Following Sentences**

(1) 冰墩墩超级抢手！

　　Bing Dwen Dwen is much sought-after.

(2) 我想买冰墩墩，但它脱销缺货了。

　　I'd like to buy Bing Dwen Dwen, but it is out of stock.

(3) 冰墩墩太抢手，一下子就卖光了。

　　Bing Dwen Dwen flew off the shelves and was quickly sold out.

Step 2　Flipped Classroom

∗ **Training Methods**

Paraphrasing

Repeating

Translation

Note-taking

∗ **Students' Scores**

Highest score：91

Average score：80.6

Lowest score：66

∗ **Key Words**

mascot 吉祥物

shell 外壳

robust 强壮

∗ **Common Problems**

(1) Bing Dwen Dwen is a panda that wears a shell made of ice.

"a shell made of ice" 翻译成"冰皮"吗？

(2) ... suggest purity and strength
"suggest"翻译成"建议"吗?
"purity"翻译成"纯净,纯粹"吗?
(3) ... means robust and lively, and represents children.
"robust"翻译成"机器人"吗?

Ⅰ. Sentence Interpreting
Beijing's cute Olympic mascot is Bing Dwen Dwen. Bing Dwen Dwen was chosen from thousands of Chinese designs in 35 countries worldwide. Bing Dwen Dwen is a panda that wears a shell made of ice. Bing means "ice" in Chinese, and is meant to suggest purity and strength. And Dwen Dwen means robust and lively, and represents children.
北京冬奥会可爱的吉祥物是冰墩墩。冰墩墩是从全球35个国家的华人设计作品中选出来的。冰墩墩是一只穿着冰晶外壳的熊猫。"冰"在中文里面代表纯洁和力量。"墩墩"寓意强壮、活泼,常代表小朋友们。

Ⅱ. Key Points Analysis
(1) Bing Dwen Dwen is a panda that wears a shell made of ice.
"shell made of ice"翻译成"冰晶外壳"或者"冰壳"都可以,但是不要翻译成"冰皮"。
(2) suggest purity and strength
"suggest"这里不要翻译成"建议",可以翻译成"代表"或"寓意"等。
"purity"这里翻译成"纯洁"较好,而不是"纯粹"。
(3) 很多同学将robust这个单词听成了robot(机器人),导致翻译错误。想想以前我们小时候喝某品牌的牛奶,上面品牌名就是Robust,联想一下小朋友喝了牛奶就强壮,所以可以将robust翻译成"强壮的"。

Step 3　Interpreting Skills (Note-taking Skills)
* **Students' Note-taking Problems**
- 记下了数字35,后面内容没有记下来,导致漏译。
- 记下了robust,但是错译成"机器人"。

课堂教学安排

<table>
<tr><td rowspan="2">课堂教学安排</td><td>

* **Group Discussion**

What do you think of this student's note-taking?

* **Note-taking Criteria**
- Arrangement of the notes
- Logic of the notes
- Proper usage of arrows and symbols

* **Comments**

Separation of the sentences（句子之间的分割线）
Usage of arrows（表示逻辑的箭头使用）

* **Suggestions**

Do not write down the whole words.
Better use more symbols and abbreviations.

* **Usage of Arrows**

↑　rise, increase, grow, expand, develop
↓　decrease, drop, go down, descend
→　lead to, go to, export to
←　come from, originate from, import from

* **箭头符号记录要点**
- 箭头符号可以表示趋势，经常用于表示数量的增加或减少；
- 前面出现过的要点，后面也可以用箭头表示重复；
- 箭头符号也可以表示各类逻辑关系，例如，表示因果；
- 在笔记教学中，要把符号系统化，不要在口译现场发明新的符号。

Step 4　Summary

脱销 out of stock
卖光 be sold out
吉祥物 mascot
外壳 shell
强壮的 robust

Step 5　Assignments

1. 第 10 组同学将 Simulation 10 上传至课程中心，第 11 组同学准备 Simulation 11。
2. 听译视频材料 *London: A City of Gaming*，将口译笔记和口译上传至在线学习中心。

Key words

Monopoly Board《大富翁》游戏
iconic 标志性的
Trafalgar square 特拉法加广场
mayor 市长
interactive entertainment 互动娱乐

</td><td>

</td></tr>
</table>

板书设计	mascot shell robust	**Note-taking Criteria** arrangement of the notes logic arrows and symbols

教学反思

Students' reflection on the course

1. Students are very interested in the topic of Bing Dwen Dwen.
2. Students find it helpful to discuss their common problems in interpretation.
3. Students think the tips for writing down the notes are very useful.

Teacher's reflection on the course

1. Note-taking is a bit challenging for the students and they need more practice in this field.
2. Students need some tips to memorize some key words. After several weeks' intensive training in note-taking, the teacher finds that many students are now more familiar with the usage of the arrows.

3. Business Interpreting: E-sports

课程名称	口译理论与实践	教学对象	英语专业三年级学生
学时安排	1学时		
教学目标	**Knowledge Objectives** 1. Know some English expressions relating to E-sports. 2. Understand the necessity of note-taking. **Ability Objectives** 1. Be able to write interpretation notes by using symbols. 2. Be able to interpret a short passage with the help of note-taking. **Emotion Objectives** 1. A growing interest in note-taking skills. 2. A new understanding of the E-sports industry.		
教学思想	The teaching of interpretation is based on the ideas of flipped classroom. Before the class, the teacher gives the students the video of *London: A City of Gaming* and asks them to upload their note-taking and their interpretation. During the class, the teacher asks them to summarize their common problems and give suggestions to each other's interpretation. After class, the teacher gives feedback to students' assignments through online learning platform and gives students one-on-one personal guidance during the weekly interpretation workshop.		
教学分析			
教学内容	Preparation before interpretation Flipped classroom: *London: A City of Gaming* Interpretation skills: note-taking		
教学重点	Know some English expressions relating to E-sports		
教学难点	Be able to write interpretation notes by using symbols		
教学方法	Flipped classroom; blended learning		
教学过程			
课堂教学安排	**Step 1　Preparation Before Interpretation** **Ⅰ. Knowledge Preparation** Thematic knowledge and language knowledge points. **Ⅱ. Listening and Translation** Distinguish the primary and secondary relations and internal relations of ideas.		

Ⅲ. Warming-up Exercise

* Sight interpretation

EDG won the 2021 League of Legend World Championship

- The hashtag #EDG is champion# had attracted 209 million viewers. The livestreaming of the championship had more than 200 million viewers on two major domestic smartphone apps, and the number was boosted by viewers on other channels.

  #EDG 是冠军#的标签已经吸引了 2.09 亿观众。本届赛事直播在国内两大智能手机应用上的收视人数均超过 2 亿,并受到其他渠道收视人数的推动。

- In 2021, E-sports events were included in the list of events of the 19th Asian Games. E-sports became an official competitive event of the Asian Games for the first time, and the scores will be included in the National Medal list.

  2021 年,电子体育项目入选第 19 届亚运会项目。电子体育项目首次成为亚运会正式竞赛项目,其成绩将计入国家奖牌榜。

* Knowledge preparation

Monopoly Board《大富翁》游戏
iconic 标志性的
Trafalgar square 特拉法加广场
mayor 市长
interactive entertainment 互动娱乐
Minecraft《我的世界》游戏

Step 2　Flipped Classroom:*London: A City of Gaming*

The London Games Festival is an annual video gaming festival for both consumers and trade specialists. The festival is part of a new initiative to boost investment.

* Students' Scores

Highest score:90
Average score:78
Lowest score:60

* Common Problems

(1) Games are taking over London.
"take over"翻译成"占领"吗?
(2) to this giant monopoly board in the iconic Trafalgar Square
"iconic"翻译成"图标的"吗?

（3）a week long celebration of tech

很多同学没有听出来"tech"。

Text

Games are taking over London from bars and exhibition halls to this giant monopoly board in the iconic Trafalgar Square, even the mayor is becoming a digital Minecraft character.

In the first ten days of April this year, London will truly become a city of gaming.

It's all part of London Games Festival, a week-long celebration of tech, interactive entertainment and of course playing games.

Key points analysis

（1）Games are taking over London.

"take over"不要翻译成"占领"，这里可以翻译成"席卷"或者"风靡"。

（2）to this giant monopoly board in the iconic Trafalgar Square

"iconic"不要翻译成"图标的"，这里可以翻译成"地标性的"或者"标志性的"（景点）。

文化知识：特拉法加广场是伦敦的一个地标性的广场，是一个著名的景点。

Step 3 Note-taking Skills

* **According to the experts, what are some guidelines in note-taking?**

- Notes supplementary short-term memory
- Develop a note-taking system that suits you
- Layout, keywords, idea reminders
- Figures

文献阅读

　　阅读《口译笔记实战指导》第二章《口译笔记研究综述》，了解口译笔记的最新研究。例如，基于口译量表的研究已经成为众多口译研究者最新关注的热点。如周金华、董燕萍（2019）基于《口译能力量表》，研发出了《口译笔记熟练量表》，他们通过研究文献、学员日志及访谈，最终完成了包括了4个维度和21个题项的《口译笔记熟练量表》。4个维度涵盖了听记协调性、笔记的时效性、笔记的系统性及笔记的利用。

<table>
<tr><td rowspan="2">课
堂
教
学
安
排</td><td>

* **Group discussion**

What do you think of this student's note-taking?

* **Strength**

The logic is clear.

The usage of arrows is good.

The usage of capital letters is nice.

* **Suggestions**

Do not write down the whole words.

Better use more symbols and abbreviations.

建议该生不要记录 weekly celebration、play games，一定要摆脱之前听写（dictation）的习惯，不要将单词记全。除此之外，该生的符号运用也可以加强，例如，熟记一些常用的符号来辅助自己记录。

* **常用口译符号**

country/state/nation □

treaty/agreement U

bilateral 2&

conflict/confrontation C ×

international/worldwide ○

meeting/conference/negotiation ⊙

important/best/outstanding/ brilliant ☆

Step 4　Summary

* **Key Words**

Monopoly Board

iconic

Trafalgar Square

mayor

interactive entertainment

Step 5　Assignments

1. 第 10 组同学将 Simulation 10 上传至课程中心，第 11 组同学准备 Simulation 11。
2. 听译视频材料，将口译笔记和口译上传至在线学习中心。
3. 预习 Unit 8 Cultural Exchange。

</td></tr>
</table>

课堂教学安排	References: 1. 胡雅楠. 口译笔记实战指导[M]. 苏州: 苏州大学出版社, 2023. 2. 周金华, 董燕萍. 口译笔记熟练度量表的开发[J]. 外语教学与研究, 2019, 51(6): 925–937, 961.	
板书设计	E-sports take over iconic	Note-taking criteria Arrangement Logic Arrows and symbols

教学反思

Students' reflection on the course

1. Students are very interested in the topic of EDG winning the world champion.
2. Students think the tips for writing down the notes are very useful and they really like the demo of the note-taking.
3. Students find the current studies on note-taking very interesting.

Teacher's reflection on the course

1. The choice of this topic attracts the attention from the students.
2. Students have an active participation in the discussion of the notes of their classmates.
3. It is very important for the teacher to provide students with some latest theoretical development in the area of interpreting skills.

4. Cultural Interpreting: Du Fu

课程名称	口译理论与实践	教学对象	英语专业三年级学生
学时安排	1学时		
教学目标	**Knowledge Objectives** 1. Know some key words relating to the documentary film on Du Fu. 2. Understand the necessity of linear interpretation. 3. Know the tips of linear interpretation. 4. Know the tips of interpreting the poems. **Ability Objectives** 1. Be able to interpret the sentences by using the tips of linear interpretation. 2. Be able to appreciate, analyze and evaluate various translated versions of some famous Chinese poems. **Emotion Objectives** 1. Increase the admiration for Du Fu and the pride in the great history of Chinese poetry. 2. Develop an interest of cross-cultural communication through the translation of poetry.		
教学思想	The teaching of interpretation is based on the ideas of flipped classroom. Before the class, the teacher gives the students the video of *Du Fu* and asks them to upload their note-taking and their interpretation on the online course platform. During the class, the teacher summarizes their common problems and discusses with them the interpretation skills of linear interpretation. After class, the teacher gives comments on students' assignments through online learning platform and give them personal guidance relating to linear interpretation.		
教学分析			
教学内容	Preparation before interpretation Flipped classroom: documentary film on Du Fu Interpreting skills: linear interpretation		
教学重点	Understand the necessity of linear interpretation The tips of interpreting the poems		
教学难点	Be able to interpret the sentences by using the linear interpretation		
教学方法	Flipped classroom; blended learning		

	教学过程
课堂教学安排	**Step 1 Preparation Before Interpretation** * **Background Knowledge of BBC Documentary Film *Du Fu*** • China has the oldest living tradition of poetry in the world, more than 3,000 years old, older than Homer's *Iliad* and *Odyssey*. 中国有着世界上最古老的、迄今仍活跃着的诗歌传统,上下延续三千年,比荷马史诗《伊利亚特》和《奥德赛》更古老。 • Born in 712, the age of *Beowulf* in Britain, Du Fu lived through the violent fall of China's brilliant Tang dynasty. There's Dante, there's Shakespeare, and there's Du Fu. 杜甫生于712年,对应于英语文学传统,那是英雄叙事长诗、古英语传说《贝奥武夫》的时代。他的一生,经历了盛唐的倾颓。在世界文学的大范围内,他可以同但丁、莎士比亚相比肩。 * **Key Points Analysis** 在翻译 *Beowulf* 的时候,需要加入文化注释。建议增加定语"英雄叙事长诗、古英语传说",从而帮助读者更好地理解这个单词。 There's Dante, there's Shakespeare, and there's Du Fu. 如果翻译成"我们有但丁、莎士比亚和杜甫",句子就没有气势。所以可翻译成"比肩",突出杜甫和但丁、莎士比亚在世界文学史上的贡献相比肩,更切合纪录片对杜甫的高度肯定。 **Step 2 Flipped Classroom** technicality 技术性细节 Roman poet Ovid 罗马诗人奥维德 prose translation 散文翻译 flavor 韵味 * **Students' Scores** Highest score: 91 Average score: 80.6 Lowest score: 66

✳ Class Activity 课堂在线问卷

How many times did you listen to the materials?

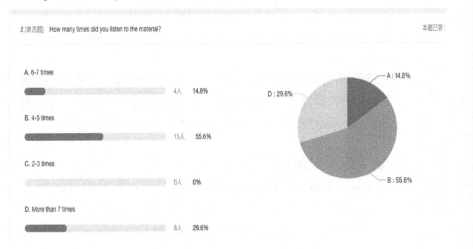

✳ Common Problems

(1) You see, film, by its very nature, is a kind of cultural exchange.
"You see"翻译成"你看"吗?
(2) We've done films in the past on the life of Shakespeare.
"do films"翻译成"做电影"吗?
(3) ... without going into the technicality of the language and the script.
"without going into"翻译成"没有进入"吗?
(4) How would we explain Du Fu?
"explain"翻译成"解释"吗?

✳ Sentence Interpreting

Text

- You see, film, by its very nature, is a kind of cultural exchange. And this was the first ever film to be made in the Western world about Du Fu, introducing the great poet of one civilization to another civilization. We've done films in the past on the life of Shakespeare. We've made a film of the great Roman poet Ovid for his two thousand anniversaries. And when we set out to do the film about Du Fu, it was really a great challenge to try to introduce Du Fu to the Western audience without going into the technicality of the language and the script.

纪录片的本质就是一种文化交流。这是西方世界第一部关于杜甫的纪录片,把一个文明世界的伟大诗人介绍给另一个文明世界。我们拍过关于莎士比亚生平的纪录片。我们还拍过一部关于伟大的罗马诗人奥维德的纪录片,为纪念他诞辰两千年。而当我们开始拍有关杜甫的纪录片时,这确实是一个很大的挑战。要把杜甫介绍给西方观众,又不拘泥于语言和文本的技巧。

- And it is, of course, a very hard thing to do. Because they are essential to the understanding of any poet. Just like you in China find when you are working on Shakespeare. How would we explain Du Fu? (How would we) give Du Fu's flavor to the Western audience? We decided to use prose translation to tell the story of his life.

  这当然是一件非常困难的事情,因为(语言和文本)关乎理解诗人的核心。就像你在中国研究莎士比亚一样。我们该如何解读杜甫?如何把杜甫的韵味传达给西方观众呢?我们决定用散文译文来讲述他的一生。

∗ **Key Points Analysis**

(1) You see, film, by its very nature, is a kind of cultural exchange.

"You see""you know"这一类没有实际意义的词都不需要翻译。

"film"要结合上下文来翻译,这里的意思是 documentary film(纪录片),而不是普通意义上的电影。

(2) We've done films in the past on the life of Shakespeare.

"do films"译成"做电影"太过生硬,应该是"拍电影"。

(3) … without going into the technicality of the language and the script.

这里"without going into"不要翻译成"不要进入",这里可意译为"不拘泥于",贴近原文的表达。

(4) How would we explain Du Fu?

"explain"可以翻译成"解释",但这里更贴切的表达可以是"解读",解读一位伟大的诗人的作品更符合我们中文的惯用表达。

(5) We've made a film of the great Roman poet Ovid for his two thousand anniversaries.

一般译法:我们还拍过一部关于伟大的罗马诗人奥维德两千年诞辰的纪录片。

顺译法:我们还拍过一部关于伟大的罗马诗人奥维德的纪录片,为纪念他两千年诞辰。

Note:有时,顺译法译出来的句子未必很符合表达习惯,但在交传和同传的场合,顺译法是译员必不可少的技能。

Step 3 Interpretation Skills:Linear Interpretation

∗ **Group Discussion:Why do we need linear interpretation?**

* **Students' Answers**

Fast！

Easy to translate！

Save time！

Reduce the memory capacity！

* **Necessity of Linear Interpretation**
- Reduce the memory capacity.
- Reduce the anxiety of the interpreters.
- Fast to interpret.

* **Tips for Linear Interpretation**

顺译是口译的重要技巧,由于英汉两种语言的差异,要想实现顺译通常需要加以辅助技巧,其中包括断句、重复、等待等。

顺译的句子有时显生硬,因此需要用汉语的衔接手段将小句子进行整合。

1. 断句:将英语句子按适当的意群进行切分。

It was really a great challenge to try to introduce Du Fu to the Western audience without going into the technicality of the language and the script.

一般译法:要把杜甫介绍给西方观众,又不拘泥于语言和文本的技巧,这确实是一个很大的挑战。

顺译法:这确实是一个很大的挑战,要把杜甫介绍给西方观众,又不拘泥于语言和文本的技巧。

2. 增加补充信息。

采用顺译法翻译进行断句时,要将分开的意群在尽可能较少移位的前提下连贯起来。"＋"表示补充信息。

The production of this documentary film on Du Fu comes on an important anniversary, as the producer mentioned.

顺译:这部杜甫纪录片的制作＋正＋逢一个重要的周年纪念,这正如制片人刚才说的＋那样。

3. 等待:通过等待后续重要信息的输入来整合小句子,斜线表示断句处。

His research on Du Fu / would not have been so successful / if he / hasn't received the support of his team members.

顺译法:他关于杜甫的研究(等待)如果没有得到(停顿)团队成员的帮助就不可能这么成功。

Step 4　Techniques of Interpreting Poems

BBC纪录片中的杜诗英译参照了历史学家洪业、英国汉学家戴维·霍克思(David Hawkes)等众多学者的译作。

1. 译者根据英文诗歌的习惯,常在诗歌中加入第二人称,将读者直接代入其中,成为诗人的同伴或倾诉对象。

故人入我梦,明我长相忆。

But you've been in my dreams as if you know how much I miss you.

恐非平生魂,路远不可测。

I feel as if you are no longer mortal, and the distance between us is so great.

2. 对于中国文化词,除了直接将其省略进行句间重组外,片中的杜诗英译也常运用对文化词做出解释和直接翻译出其文化内涵的方式来处理。

开口咏凤凰。

My first poem was about the phoenix, the harbinger of a sagacious reign, a new age of wisdom.

饮酣视八极,俗物都茫茫。

Exhilarated by wine, we cast our glances over the entire universe; and all vulgar worldliness dwindled into oblivion.

Step 5　Summary

伟大的诗歌有超越语言和文化的力量,因其探讨的是永恒的人之本性。

Great poetry has the power to transcend culture and language because it deals with eternal human truths.

Step 6　Assignments

1. 第11组同学将Simulation 11上传至课程中心,第12组同学准备Simulation 12。
2. 继续听译杜甫纪录片下半部分,将口译录音和口译笔记上传至在线学习中心。
3. 预习Unit 14 Vocabulary。

References:

[1] 邓媛,朱健平,张威.交替传译认知加工焦虑量表的编制及其效度检验[J].外语教学与研究,2018(3):451-462,481.

[2] 吴文梅.口译记忆训练模型APEC Model构建[J].上海翻译,2017(2):74-78.

板书设计	you see do films without going into explain	**Linear Interpretation** Necessity Reduce the memory capacity! Reduce the stress! Fast!
教学反思		

Students' reflection on the course

1. Students find translating the background information of the documentary film on Du Fu is very helpful to their later interpretation.

2. Students find doing linear interpretation during this stage is still a bit challenging and needs more practice after class.

Teacher's reflection on the course

1. Interpreting poems with cultural elements is a bit difficult for the students. For this class, the teacher selects BBC's documentary film on Du Fu as the interpreting material, and the feedback from the students is very good. Students find it very interesting to see how westerners interpret the poems of Du Fu.

2. It is novel to compare the poems of Du Fu with those of William Shakespeare. The cross-cultural exchange of the poems is inspiring.

5. Cultural Interpreting: Father of Hybrid Rice

课程名称	口译理论与实践	教学对象	英语专业三年级学生
学时安排	1学时		
教学目标	**Knowledge Objectives** 1. Know some key words relating to hybrid rice. 2. Know some techniques of linear interpretation. **Ability Objectives** Be able to interpret the sentences by using the skills of linear interpretation. **Emotion Objectives** Develop an admiration for Yuan Longping and show respect for him.		
教学思想	The teaching of interpretation is based on the ideas of flipped classroom. Before the class, the teacher gives the students the video of *Father of Hybrid Rice* and asks them to upload their note-taking and their interpretation on the online course platform. During the class, the teacher summarizes their common problems and discusses with them the necessity and tips for linear interpretation. After class, the teacher gives comments on students' assignment through online learning platform.		
教学分析			
教学内容	Preparation before interpretation Flipped classroom: *Father of Hybrid Rice* Interpretation skills: linear interpretation		
教学重点	Understand the necessity and the skills of linear interpretation		
教学难点	Interpret the sentences by using the skills of linear interpretation		
教学方法	Flipped classroom; blended learning		
教学过程			
课堂教学安排	**Step 1 Preparation Before Interpretation** * **Background Information** 　　Yuan Longping helped China to work a great wonder—feeding nearly one-fifth of the world's population with less than 9 percent of the world's total land. 　　Yuan's remarkable achievements in hybrid rice research have won him numerous awards including China's State Supreme Science and Technology Award. 　　Yuan Longping made two major discoveries in hybrid rice cultivation, which helped to increase harvest steeply and put an end to famine in most of the world.		

* Vocabulary

袁隆平倾其一生研究水稻,他的名字在中国家喻户晓,他被亲切地称为"杂交水稻之父"。即便在晚年,袁隆平也未曾停止研究。在杂交水稻领域,中国在领跑。

Yuan Longping spent his life researching rice and was a **household name** in China, known by the nickname **Father of Hybrid Rice**. Even in his **later years**, Mr. Yuan did not stop doing research. It was China who **led the game** afterward.

Step 2　Flipped Classroom：Yuan Longping's Interview

* Key Words

- the Food and Agriculture Organization of the United Nations
  联合国粮食及农业组织
- super-hybrid rice
  超级杂交水稻

* Students' Scores

Highest score：91
Average score：80.6
Lowest score：66

* Common Problems

(1) spread in dozens of countries
"spread"翻译成"散布"吗?
(2) exploring new areas of super-hybrid rice
"explore"翻译成"考察"吗?
(3) As long as my life is going on …
翻译成"只要我的生活还在继续"是否妥当?

原文和译文:

- The Food and Agriculture Organization of the United Nations once asked you six times to be their chief consultant.
  联合国粮食及农业组织曾六次聘请您担任首席顾问。
- I don't want to hide the fact. I have many titles both in China and abroad.
  我不想回避这些事实,我的确在国内外有很多头衔。
- But this one I value it very much.
  但我对这个非常重视。

- To train the talent for all countries, especially for developing countries is one of my life-long wishes.

  为各国培养优秀人才,尤其是为发展中国家,这是我一生的愿望。

- Your hybrid rice is famous all over the world and spread in dozens of countries on a large scale.

  您的杂交水稻闻名世界,在许多国家广为推广。

- How do you feel about that?

  您对此有何感想?

- Of course, I am very happy and excited.

  当然,我很高兴和激动。

- Because hybrid rice technology not only belongs to China, but also to the whole world.

  我的杂交水稻技术不仅属于中国,也属于全世界。

- Are you still exploring new areas of super-hybrid rice?

  您还在探索超级杂交水稻这个新领域吗?

- As long as my life is going on, I never stop pursuing and dreaming for super-hybrid rice.

  生命不息,我将继续追寻超级杂交水稻之梦。为了梦想,永不停歇。

* **Key Points Analysis**

(1) spread in dozens of countries …

"spread"不要翻译成"散布",这里结合上下文,可以翻译成"推广"。

(2) exploring new areas of super-hybrid rice …

"explore"更多的含义是"探究",这里可以翻译成"探索"。

(3) As long as my life is going on …

"只要我的生活还在继续",直译的感觉太直白,无法体现原文的意境,建议用更诗意的语言来体现中文的意境,例如,可翻译为"生命不息",蕴含"生生不息、探索不止"的深意。

* **Extended Information**

- 他们说,我用一粒种子改变了世界。我知道,这粒种子,是妈妈您在我幼年时种下的!

People say I've changed the world with one tiny rice seed but mom. I know you sowed the seed in me when I was a little boy.

- Yuan Longping's Mom

Born in a wealthy merchant family in Yangzhou, Hua Jing was well educated and open-minded.

She taught Yuan English when he was very young. Having never worked in the fields, Hua moved to Anjiang Town to support her son's family and research.

∗ **顺译练习**

妈妈,每当我的研究取得成果,我总是对人说,这辈子对我影响最深的人就是妈妈您啊!我无法想象,没有您的英语启蒙,在一片闭塞中,我怎么能够阅读世界上最先进的科学文献。

Mom, whenever I get progress in my scientific research, I always talk to others that the person who has the greatest impact on me is you!

I can't imagine, without your English enlightenment, how could I read the most advanced scientific literature in that secluded environment?

Step 3 Interpreting Skills

∗ **Group Discussion**

What are the skills of linear interpretation?

∗ **Tips for Linear Interpretation**

顺译是同声传译的重要技巧,由于英汉两种语言的差异,要想实现顺译通常需要加以辅助技巧,其中包括等待、断句、重复、转换、预测等。断句指的是将英语句子按适当的意群进行切分。顺译的句子有时生硬,因此,需要用汉语的衔接手段将小句子进行整合。

1. 采用顺译法翻译时,要将分开的意群在尽可能较少移位的前提下连贯起来,示例如下,用"＋"表示补充信息。

- Yuan Longping graduated from Southwest Agricultural College in China in 1953, and then was assigned to teach crop genetics and breeding at an agricultural school in Hunan Province.

  顺译法:袁隆平1953年毕业于中国的西南农学院,之后讲授作物遗传和育种课程,＋(在)湖南省的一所农业学校＋(工作)。

- To train the talent for all countries, especially for developing countries, is one of my life-long wishes.

| | 一般译法：我一生的愿望是为各国，尤其是为发展中国家培养优秀人才。
顺译法：为各国，尤其为发展中国家培养优秀人才，这是我一生的愿望。

2. 断句法：将英语句子按适当的意群进行切分。
Farmers in more than ten other countries have thus benefited from his work, gaining access to the new technology/they may otherwise never have imagined.
顺译法：十多个国家的农民因此受益于他的工作，获得了新技术，+ 这是他们之前无法想象的。

3. 等待法：通过等待后续重要信息的输入来整合小句子。
His research on hybrid rice / would not have been so successful / if he / hasn't received the support of his team members.
顺译法：他关于杂交水稻的研究（等待）如果没有得到（停顿）团队成员的帮助就不可能这么成功。

Step 4　Summary
* **Key Words**
杂交水稻之父 Father of Hybrid Rice
家喻户晓 household name
大幅增产 increase harvest steeply
消除饥饿 put an end to famine
联合国粮食及农业组织 the Food and Agriculture Organization of the United Nations

顺译通常需要加以辅助技巧，其中包括等待、断句、重复、转换、预测等。

Step 5　Assignments
1. 第12组同学将 Simulation 12 上传至课程中心，第13组同学准备 Simulation 13。
2. 听译视频材料 *Touching China 2020 National Prize*，将口译笔记和口译上传至在线学习中心。
live up to the school's ideals 践行学校的理想
take one's toll 遭受损伤
long-held beliefs 长期坚持的信念 |
|---|---|

(左侧纵排：课堂教学安排)

板书设计	Father of Hybrid Rice increase harvest steeply put an end to famine household name lead the game	**Linear Interpretation** **Tips** Separate Add Wait
教学反思			

Students' reflection on the course

- Students find the story of Yuan Longping very moving and touching.
- Having learnt the tips for linear interpretation for several weeks, many students gradually develop the habit of doing interpretation in a linear manner.

Teacher's reflection on the course

The teacher chose the listening material of Yuan Longping and shared with the students Yuan's contribution to China. The teacher found that this material is very inspiring and can touch the students. In terms of students' interpretation skills, some of them have acquired the skills of linear interpretation by using separating, adding and waiting techniques.

6. Cultural Interpreting: Buzzwords

课程名称	口译理论与实践	教学对象	英语专业三年级学生
学时安排	1学时		
教学目标	**Knowledge Objectives** 1. Know the translation for some popular buzzwords. 2. Understand the implied meaning for the buzzwords. 3. Understand the tips of number interpreting. **Ability Objectives** Be able to interpret the numbers correctly. **Emotion Objectives** 1. Develop a desire to become an interpreter in the future. 2. Show respect to everyday heroes who put their duty before their lives.		
教学思想	The teaching of interpretation is based on the ideas of flipped classroom. Before the class, the teacher gives the students the video of *Buzzwords in China* and asks them to upload their note-taking and their interpretation on the online course platform. During the class, the teacher summarizes their common problems and discusses with them the interpretation skills. After class, the teacher gives feedback to students' performance through online teaching platform.		
教学分析			
教学内容	Preparation before interpretation Consecutive interpretation: Buzzwords in China Interpreting skills: interpreting numbers		
教学重点	Understand the implied meaning for the buzzwords		
教学难点	Be able to interpret the numbers correctly		
教学方法	Flipped classroom; blended learning		
教学过程			

课堂教学安排

Step 1　Preparation Before Interpretation

＊ **Background Information**

- 内卷 involution: A buzzword meaning irrational or involuntary competition, which makes people feel burned out

  "内卷"指非理性内部竞争,或是非自愿竞争,让人极度劳累。

● 躺平 lie flat

It describes the people who have little ambition and do the bare minimum to get by. Some people think lying flat is a passive choice in a fast-changing society and some believe this is just to vent stress before they get going again.

"躺平"是指一些人放弃奋斗、低欲望生活。有人认为躺平是对社会快速发展的选择。有人认为躺平是为了释放情绪后更好地前进。

● 逆行者 heroes in harm's way

Heroes in harm's way refers to everyday heroes such as medical professionals, military personnel and firefighters.

"逆行者"是指那些不惧风险、无私奉献的人物群体。例如,医护工作者、解放军、消防员等。

* **Sight Interpretation**

The buzzwords reflect the changing and unchanging elements in our values as China experiences rapid economic growth and profound social transformation.

我们正处在中国经济快速发展和社会深刻变革过程中,这些热词反映的是价值取向的变与不变。

Step 2 Flipped Classroom: Buzzwords

Ⅰ. Preparation Before Interpretation

* **Key Words**

mobilize resources 调集资源

epic 史诗般的

be united as one 团结一致

* **Scores for the Previous Assignment**

Highest Score: 92

Average Score: 81

Lowest Score: 75

* **Common Problems**

(1) We mobilized resources nationwide.

"mobilized resources nationwide"翻译成"移动全国的资源"吗?

(2) ... with no place left behind and no life given up.

"with no place left behind"翻译成"没有一个地方被遗忘"吗?

(3) When COVID-19 hit China ...

"hit"翻译成"打击"吗?

II. Sentence Interpreting

People first, life first, this phrase was from China's fight against the pandemic.

When COVID-19 hit China, we mobilized resources nationwide and launched an epic campaign to fight it. The whole country was united as one, with no place left behind and no life given up.

From a 30-hour-old baby to senior citizens of over 100 years old, no cost was spared to save a life, and all the treatment was free.

"人民至上,生命至上",这句话来自中国抗击疫情时期。

当新冠疫情肆虐时,我们调集了全国资源,打了一场史诗级抗疫之战。举国同心,不放弃每一个角落,不放弃每一个生的希望。

从出生仅30个小时的婴儿到百岁老人,我们不惜一切代价拯救生命,而且所有的医疗都是免费的。

III. Key Points Analysis

(1) We mobilized resources nationwide.

"mobilize"不要翻译成"移动",这里可以翻译成"调集"。"调集全国资源"更符合习惯表达。

(2) … with no place left behind and no life given up.

有同学翻译成"没有一个地方被遗忘",显然是错误的,可译成"不放弃每一个角落"。

"with no …"开头的短语,一定要将后面的意群听清楚,再进行翻译,并注意语句连贯。例如"with no child left behind"可翻译成"不让每一个孩子掉队"。

(3) When COVID-19 hit China …

"hit"原意是"打击",这里可翻译成"肆虐"。

同学们口译的时候,经常会下意识使用单词的本来意思。

建议同学们将一些看似简单的动词的口译做个整理,学习不同场合这类动词的固定搭配和相关翻译。

Step 3 Interpreting Skills: Note-taking
Group Discussion

What do you think of this student's note-taking?

* Strength

Write down the key information.

重点记录到位。

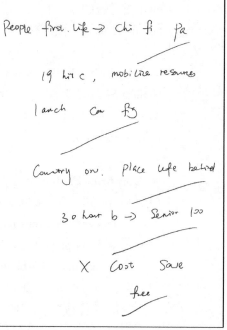

Write down the numbers.
数字记录清晰。
Separation of the sentences.
句子之间的分割线清晰。

* **Suggestions**
Do not write down the whole words.
Better use more symbols.
建议不要写全单词,例如,笔记中出现的 people、first、life,在记录笔记的时候,一定要学会用单词的前两三个字母进行记录。在这篇笔记中,该生对数字的记录较为准确。同时,结合之前所学的口译符号,建议该生可以多运用一些常用符号来节省记录时间。

Step 4　The Skills of Number Interpreting

阿拉伯数字	英语	汉语
1	one	一
10	ten	十
100	one hundred	一百
1,000	one thousand	一千
10,000	ten thousand	一万
100,000	one hundred thousand	十万
1,000,000	one million	一百万
10,000,000	ten million	一千万
100,000,000	one hundred million	一亿
1,000,000,000	one billion	十亿
10,000,000,000	ten billion	一百亿
100,000,000,000	one hundred billion	一千亿
1,000,000,000,000	one trillion	一兆(万亿)

* 数字记录方法
Ⅰ. 缩略语记录法
K：Thousand
M：Million
Bn：Billion

课堂教学安排	Ⅱ．分节号记录法 ，Thousand ，，Million ，，，Billion Ⅲ．点线记录法 四亿八千零九万 480,090,000 Ⅳ．小数点记录法 13亿 1.3 bn ＊**Practise**（为突出数字的口译，译文中的数字用汉字表示） （1）The population of this city in 2004 was 78,872,890. 该城市2004年的人口是七千八百八十七万二千八百九十人。 （2）The natural reserve takes up an area of 123,880,000 square kilometers. 自然保护区占地一亿两千三百八十八万平方千米。 **Step 5　Assignments** 1. 复习Note-taking部分，整理前8次口译笔记，并写好反思笔记。 2. 听译视频材料 *Yang Jiechi's 15-minute Remarks at the China-US Alaska Summit*，将口译笔记和口译上传至在线学习中心。 3. 从在线题库选取"数字口译"练习进行课后练习。 References： 1. 李晋，张威，陈文荣. 交替传译笔记的视觉语法对译员口译产出质量影响研究［J］. 外语与外语教学，2022（4）：36－47，146. 2. 吴钟明. 英语口译笔记法实战指导（3版）［M］. 武汉：武汉大学出版社，2017.	
板书设计	buzzwords mobilize hit with no place left behind	Number Interpreting 1. 缩略语记录法 2. 分节号记录法 3. 点线记录法 4. 小数点记录法

教学反思

Students' reflection on the course

1. Many students find number interpreting very difficult.
2. Many of the students have improved note-taking in terms of separation of the sense group and the usage of arrows.

Teacher's reflection on the course

1. According to students' feedback, number interpreting is very difficult for them. Therefore, students need more practice in this field.
2. Students' note-taking shows what many students have improved in terms of the separation of the sense group, which shows that they have a better grasp of the logic of their notes. Besides, many of them have developed their own note-taking systems.